Mere Apologetics
Using the Apostles' Creed to Defend the Faith

by Matthew Bertels

Mere Apologetics: Using the Apostles' Creed to Defend the Faith

Trilogy Christian Publishers A Wholly Owned Subsidary of Trinity Broadcasting Network

2442 Michelle Drive Tustin, CA 92780

Cover design by: Grant Swank

For information about special discounts for bulk purchases, please contact Trilogy Christian Publishing.

Trilogy Disclaimer: The views and content expressed in this book are those of the author and may not necessarily reflect the views and doctrine of Trilogy Christian Publishing or the Trinity Broadcasting Network.

Manufactured in the United States of America

10 9 8 7 6 5 4 3 2 1

Library of Congress Cataloging-in-Publication Data is available.

ISBN: 978-1-68556-117-8

E-ISBN: 978-1-68556-118-5

Dedication

To Rachael. I can never thank you enough for all of your love and support and for introducing me to your best friend, Jesus.

Table of Contents

Preface...5

Chapter 1. I Believe...7

Chapter 2. God...15

Chapter 3. Creator...25

Chapter 4. Jesus Christ...37

Chapter 5. Christmas Story...53

Chapter 6. Suffered..67

Chapter 7. He Is Risen..81

Chapter 8. Descended and Ascended......................................99

Chapter 9. Holy Spirit..107

Chapter 10. Scary Words...121

The Ending...133

About the Author..147

Bibliography...148

Endnotes..149

Preface

It was a Sunday like any other Sunday. We were getting ready for our standard worship service. About two months earlier, I had instituted reciting the Apostles' Creed before the service. It was something that I had seen as having been used in the early church while I was finishing my major writing project at Trinity Theological Seminary on the use of Augustine in countering heresy in the church today, so I thought it would be something to close the gap between what is taught in the church and what we are, as Christians, obligated to believe. As we began reciting the creed, I heard a young voice standing out from all of the other voices in the congregation. It was a voice I was accustomed to hearing, as it was my third child's, just not at this point in the service. I stopped reciting the creed myself and just listened, as a three-year-old was reciting the creed without error. It moved me in a way that I was not prepared for. After it was done, I talked about why the creed was important, almost talking to my three-year-old son in a way that was reassuring and showing that I was proud of his accomplishment.

This was the point that I decided that this book was necessary. There are hundreds of books on apologetics in this world. I have read many of them. There are also hundred of books on the Apostles' Creed. I have also read many of them. This book is supposed to be a conglomeration of these two types of books. It seeks to show that we, as believers in Jesus, can *know* that what we believe is true and can hold to the creed fundamentally. It is also a beacon to those who have strayed from the tenets of the Apostles' Creed to come back. This is a call to stop straying so far from what the church has held to for two thousand years and decide that they will follow Jesus, the way that the church has followed Him since its genesis. I pray that this work will help to guide those who are seeking to know if Christianity is true to the conclusion that it is indeed. While this book is not the be-all and end-all of text regarding either of these topics, my hope is that it will be helpful to a generation that is seeking answers to life's toughest questions.

Chapter 1

I Believe

When looking at the history of the church, one should first look at what the church believes. Creeds have been a part of the church since its genesis, starting with the creed that Paul records in 1 Corinthians 15:3–6. Skeptics such as Richard Carrier and Bart Ehrman have both stated that this creed has been around since the dawn of the Christian faith. This creed was believed to be what Paul was preaching when he was beginning to tell people about the Messiah and continued to be a staple to his preaching ministry throughout the Roman Empire in the first century. As we see that creeds on the whole have been largely important in the foundation of the church, it can certainly be seen that the fathers of the faith believed in these formulas for showing people who were new to the faith what exactly it is that the Christian believes.

The early church ran largely off creedal statements due to the large illiteracy, with some estimates being as high as 90 percent. This would continue as the church became more literate because members of the church would be fluent in reading and writing in their local tongue while being largely unable to read Latin, the language of the Catholic Church. These creeds would provide an outline of what was said within the Bible, mostly focusing on the writings of the New Testament. These could not be separated from the Scriptures, regardless of how many people have tried to do this throughout history, because the teachings do not make sense without depth. Creeds are seen starting early in the church and continually became more detailed to keep heresy away. The focus is lost every time the creed becomes more detailed, so the focus of the church should turn back even further to get to the first fully-formed creed after the ones contained in Scripture, the Apostles' Creed.

The word creed comes from the Latin word credo, which means "I believe." The use of this term or *symbolum*, which means "symbol," was prevalent in the writings of the church fathers to describe the creeds that were held as the standards for the short form of what Christians are to believe to be considered "in the faith." As one investigates the first two hundred years of the church, the formation of the Apostles' Creed can be seen in the writings of many of the early church fathers, such as Irenaeus, Ignatius, and Tertullian. The writings all show the same formation of the Trinity within the writing and continue to show some of the ancillary beliefs that should be held for one to consider himself in the faith. These early compositions show what the faith was in the first and second centuries, and with a God that is unchanging, those things which are required to be believed by those espousing the faith should also be unchanging.

Rule of Faith

Irenaeus first delineated the proto-Creed in his text against the gnostic heresies that were varied and beginning to show up all over the known world. In his text, *Against Heresies*, he shows the creed as being an essential bit of data that the Christian can use to determine whether the teachings that are being heard are good or not. He wrote (hereinafter, all grammar and spelling has been left unedited):

> Believing in one God, the Creator of heaven and earth, and all things therein, by means of Christ Jesus, the Son of God; who, because of His surpassing love towards His creation, condescended to be born of the virgin, He Himself uniting man through Himself to God, and having suffered under Pontius Pilate, and rising again, and having been received up in splendour, shall come in glory, the Saviour of those who are saved, and the Judge of those who are judged, and sending into eternal fire those who transform the truth, and despise His Father and His advent.[1]

While the Apostles' Creed that we have today is not the exact creed that was first set forth in the mid to late second century by Irenaeus. Today's creed states all that was found in the earlier creeds, with several additions made somewhere around AD 400, which can be seen through the writings of Ambrose and Augustine. The major additions to the Creed would be the addition of the line regarding God being the Creator of heaven and earth. Historians regarding the early church, however, do regard the Apostles' Creed that we have today as one of the "daughter" creeds to have come out of the Roman Symbol, which would initially be a question and response between the pastor and the individual being baptized, which showed the need for the creed to be in the form of the Trinity.

As one looks at the history of the creed, it becomes rapidly apparent that there was a major push to get a standard set of beliefs to the general populace to counter any false teachings that would attempt to influence the believers. The initial creed appears to have been formulated as a response to Marcion and the Gnostics, who had managed to spread mistruths about what the Scriptures taught. Justo Gonzalez writes, "Marcion posed an even greater threat to the church than did the Gnostics. Like them, he rejected or radically reinterpreted the doctrines of creation, incarnation, and resurrection."[2] This showed the leaders of the church that the heresy that was attempting to infect the church must have been cut off at the pass and brought into submission. This was the initial call for a set of credal beliefs to be brought forth for all to know and understand.

This would not be the only creed to come to being due to heretical beliefs, as the creed that would come from the Council of Nicaea would be set forth to counter the false teachings of Arius that would die out for a time, yet would find a resurgence with the advent of the Jehovah's Witness organization in the late 1800s. Augustine would write succinctly that heresy was the main reason for all learning the creed and being able to recite it. He said:

It is underneath these few words, therefore, which
are thus set in order in the Creed, that most heretics
have endeavored to conceal their poisons; whom
divine mercy has withstood, and still withstands, by
the instrumentality of spiritual men, who have been
counted worthy not only to accept and believe the
catholic faith as expounded in those terms, but also
thoroughly to understand and apprehend it by the
enlightenment imparted by the Lord.[3]

The cause for needing to learn the Creed as well as the background
information that goes into the Creed is then so that one can fight
against heresy, which is why one must know what the Creed is, as well
as what is taught in it. The importance is not only in knowing what is
believed in the church but also why it is to be believed. This allows for
the creed to not only serve to edify the believer but also to strengthen
their faith, as well as serve as an evangelistic tool for those who are in
the faith with those who do not believe. This three-fold usage of the
Creed is important in the walk of every believer so that all who are
called to follow Christ can do so believing the essential doctrines that
are taught. This book will seek to break down the creed word by word
to gain the greatest understanding of what was being passed down
so that there is less confusion as to what was believed by those who
established the burgeoning faith that is now practiced by billions of
people around the globe.

Old Roman Symbol

The Old Roman Symbol was a question and response format
that was used in the early church in what is known as a tripartite
structure (modeled after the baptismal formula). This was one of the
earliest creeds to take shape. J. N. D. Kelly stated in his seminal work
on the early creeds, "The descent of the Roman creed can be traced
with some degree of confidence to the second century, at any rate

to the closing decades."[4] This means that this is a predecessor to the Apostles' Creed, which served as a baptismal question and answer for early believers and was chronicled as the rule of faith in the writings of Irenaeus and Tertullian. Coming from one of the foremost scholars regarding the church fathers, this shows that there is a certain amount of credence that should be placed on the importance of the creeds in the early church for the establishment of the basic tenets of the faith. The primacy of the Roman Symbol in the development of the Apostles' Creed should be noted when one discusses the creed and the necessity of these tenets in the church today.

Trinity

Unlike the Athanasian Creed, this creed does not explicitly state that there is a belief in the Triune God of Scripture; however, there are earmarks that show that this is a proper understanding of the Creed. In each spot where "I believe" is stated, it should be noted that these are the different persons of the Trinity that are being proclaimed. This is what a right belief in the God of the Bible is. We are not to confuse the persons of the Trinity, as each has its own role in the salvation of the believer, though there is overlap. The Athanasian Creed fully fleshes out what right belief in the Trinity looks like, though this Creed does lend itself to understanding that the Trinity is an essential belief for the Christian. In the three portions where I believe it is mentioned, the text is setting these statements apart as special in the formation of what must be believed by those who profess the Christian faith.

The Creed

While there are a variety of translations of the creed, this is the one that will be used throughout the book here. There are many keywords that can be debated, and this will cover some of these different views. The problem will be with reconciling the definitions of these words, and while some of these words are scary (see the chapter on scary words), these words will be dealt with in a way that brings light to what is meant by these words. The Apostles' Creed reads as follows:

> I believe in God, the Father almighty, creator of heaven and earth.
> I believe in Jesus Christ, his only Son, our Lord.
> He was conceived by the power of the Holy Spirit and born of the virgin Mary.
> He suffered under Pontius Pilate, was crucified, died, and was buried.
> He descended to the dead. On the third day he rose again.
> He ascended into heaven and is seated at the right hand of the Father.
> He will come again to judge the living and the dead.
> I believe in the Holy Spirit,
> the holy catholic Church,
> the communion of the saints,
> the forgiveness of sins,
> the resurrection of the body,
> and the life everlasting. Amen.

I hope that you will remain in the book long enough for some of these words to be explained and for the reason for them being included here. As this is one of the longest-standing creeds for the church, this writer does not feel at liberty to change these words in any way but to leave what has been passed down from the early church to us now. The first portion that must be discussed, though, is the word "believe."

I Believe

When looking at the word, I believe it helps to identify what the word means in Greek. (The word in the Greek text is *pisteuo*). This word means to have confidence in the truth of something. It does not mean to simply close one's eyes and take another's word for it. It means that there is a certain amount of trust that what has been read is true and that this in some way will impact the life of the believer. As the church has strayed away (slowly at first, but it's picking up steam), this word has morphed into a new meaning that Christians have allowed society to force upon it. The fact of the matter is that Jesus directed His disciples to believe from what they had been witness to. He said that there would be those who were not witnesses that would be more blessed for not having seen these events yet still believing. This does not mean that the Christian is to dismiss any evidence for the faith but is to embrace it and seek to find even more, so they can be sure of what they believe.

John wrote,

> Therefore many other signs Jesus also performed in the presence of the disciples, which are not written in this book; but these have been written so that you may believe that Jesus is the Christ, the Son of God; and that believing you may have life in His name.
>
> John 20:30–31[5]

This shows that the disciples anticipated that people would need evidence of the extraordinary things that were happening while Jesus was walking on this earth, and thus they left the believer of today with a plethora of stories that show who God is and why He sent His Son to the earth. To say that there is no importance to what one believes is to completely misplace what God has done for the believer, and to shred apart several key verses about why the text was written. We must understand that our belief is more than a mere knowledge but is a trust in the person of Jesus Christ.

Once it is understood what exactly the biblical sense of the word is, it then becomes important to see whether or not one must believe firmly each and every portion of what is being spoken of in the creed so that the believer can be firmly established in what is going on throughout the text of the Scriptures as well as what is being taught throughout the text of the creed. It is important for everyone to understand what words mean before trusting in it; therefore, it is of the utmost importance that it is understood what exactly one is talking about with regards to each of the parts of the creed. This is how one ensures that they are believing in something that is logical and makes the best sense of the world around them. These keystones are integral in continuing to walk in the Christian faith.

Content

This book will take a different shape for the rest of it. Each chapter, which will be one of the key statements made in the Creed, will begin with what an early church father stated that the church taught, followed by what the Creed states. These will be backed up by information that can be used to bolster the defense that this provides to each person that encounters someone teaching contrary to the Creed. The end of the chapter will provide a brief recap of all that was discussed throughout the pages contained therein. I pray that this venture will help you to better understand the Gospel message and that by the end, you will be able to better stand against those who would oppose it.

Chapter 2

God

The first major belief that is presented by the creed is that of God. There are many who will say that there is no way to prove that something, such as God, does not exist. This is untrue, yet, the point is not nearly as important as looking at the fact that there is ample evidence for the existence of God. There have been many throughout the course of history who have provided their own inputs into the debate that centers around whether or not God exists. There have been books of greater numbers than can be discussed here on each side of this debate, but the debate continues to rage on. The goal throughout this will be to show that God does indeed exist. This will be done by looking at the four main arguments for His existence while providing a brief history of each. These arguments do not bring you to the Father portion of the statement but will serve to merely show that God is present.

Teleological Argument

The teleological argument for the existence of God shows that the believer gives credence to there being order in the universe. "Telos," the first portion of the word, means order, so this means that there is an order to what can be seen. This thought is found throughout the Bible, but in the book of Romans, Paul gives the most succinct answer to the question of order when he wrote,

> For since the creation of the world His invisible attributes, His eternal power and divine nature, have been clearly seen, being understood through what has been made, so that they are without excuse.
>
> Romans 1:20

This means that if something is designed, one would see an expected amount of order.

The position of the one asserting that the teleological argument is true is one regarding design, which makes it difficult to not spill over into creation (that will be covered in a later chapter). William Paley, a British theologian towards the end of the eighteenth century and the beginning of the nineteenth century, made one of the most popular level arguments for the teleological argument in his book *Natural Theology: or, Evidences of the Existence and Attributes of the Deity; Collected from the Appearances of Nature*. In the book, he discussed how if one were walking through the forest and stubbed your toe on a rock, you would have no reason to assert that the rock had always been there but that it had been put there at some point in the finite past. He then asserts that if the stone were a watch, one would understand that it had not been there forever, regardless of one's knowledge about watches. He goes on to further assert that all one has to do is to look at the intricate design of the watch to understand that the watch had a maker. If the watch then had a maker and it is much more simplistic than the universe, then the more complex universe must have had a maker.

This argument is often tackled for its simplicity and has been at the center of the discussion between those who assert that the theory of evolution is true and those who hold to the creationist account of the Bible (whether old earth creation or new earth creation). The problem is that the works of Paley here do not go into the depth of the human body or the absolute intricacies of the universe. He tackles this objection in the work, saying,

> Every indication of contrivance, every manifestation of design, which existed in the watch, exists in the works of nature; with the difference, on the side of nature, of being greater or more, and that in a degree which exceeds all computation.[6]

The improbability of even one planet bringing forth life in the universe rests on many key factors that cause the probability of life to be effectively zero, if not for the appearance of design. There have been many who have attacked the design as being imperfect, citing that there is shoddy craftsmanship. This can be compared to buying a television that does not work. Just because it does not work, does that then mean that it was not designed by someone and built? This would be absurd, so this argument, clever as those making the argument believe it to be, holds no weight.

The question that should be answered here is what did the church fathers believe with regards to the design of the world? Did they see the design, or were they merely evolutionists in waiting?

Irenaeus wrote:

> That God is the Creator of the world is accepted even by those very persons who in many ways speak against Him, and yet acknowledge Him, styling Him the Creator...—all men, in fact, consenting to this truth: the ancients on their part preserving with special care, from the tradition of the first-formed man, this persuasion, while they celebrate the praises of one God, the Maker of heaven and earth; others, again, after them, being reminded of this fact by the prophets of God, while the very heathen learned it from creation itself.[7]

While this is only the opinion of this one church father, many others wrote sentiments that closely resemble this, which will be discussed much more in-depth with regards to the attribute that is given to God as the Creator of everything. It is important to understand for these purposes that the church fathers, by and large, did appeal to the teleological argument for the existence of God and did not give attributes to God that did not exist throughout the Bible. This argument still stands in use today, and many see no reason to stop using it, despite impassioned pleas from those who present that there is no God who will state that this argument has been thoroughly refuted.

Ontological Argument

The basis for the ontological argument can be found in Exodus, Chapter 3, and throughout the book of John. This argument is one that comes from the state of being (this is what ontology is the study of) and was posited in its popular form by Anselm in his *Proslogion*. The basis for the case comes as Moses is talking with God, who has taken the form of the burning bush. He asks who he should say has sent him, and God replies to him, "I AM WHO I AM"; and He said, "Thus you shall say to the sons of Israel, 'I AM has sent me to you'" (Exodus 3:14). The writer of Exodus (Moses by tradition) has shown here that God attests to His own existence using a form of the ontological argument. In stating his argument (which is really his prayer to God), Anselm wrote:

> And certainly that greater than which cannot be understood cannot exist only in thought, for if it exists only in thought it could also be thought of as existing in reality as well, which is greater. If, therefore, that than which greater cannot be thought exists in thought alone, then that than which greater cannot be thought turns out to be that than which something greater actually can be thought, but that is obviously impossible. Therefore something than which greater cannot be thought undoubtedly exists both in thought and in reality.[8]

Modern philosophers Alvin Plantinga and William Lane Craig have posited this in much the same way using the Socratic method of logical formulas. In doing this, they have updated the terminology to allow for maximal effectiveness in showing that if one can conceive of God, then He exists in the mind. The only greater thing than the existence of God in the mind is His existence in reality, which means that He must indeed exist in reality. This pattern has been widely attacked, generally using the Bible to serve as the defeater where they cite the psalmist who wrote, "The fool has said in his heart, 'There is no God'" (Psalm 14:1). They say if one can say to himself that there is no God, there are those who cannot conceive of a God; thus, they do not conceive of a maximally great being.

The ontology of Christ came into question in the third century by a bishop named Arius, who stated that Jesus was a created being who was used by the Father to fulfill His desires. This demotes Jesus from being who He and His disciples claimed He was demoting Him to the ranks of a mere mortal. While many will state that the reason for the Council of Nicaea in 325 was to determine the books of the Bible, the reason was actually to determine what doctrines were to govern the church, including this new teaching by Arius and his followers. These teachings were condemned as they did not fit with any of the teachings of the Bible and were against the teachings of the ante-Nicaean fathers. The point was that God has always been a Trinitarian God and that He has never changed. This ontology also shows that Jesus is one of the three persons of the Godhead and has never ceased to be. While the ontological argument is multi-faceted, it can be seen that what it is attempting to prove, that God exists because He necessarily must exist, succeeds in showing that there is indeed a God.

Moral Argument

Continuing to evaluate the evidence for God's existence leads one to the moral argument. This is also useful in combating the argument of evil but is known to show that even debating that one knows that evil exists shows that there is a basic understanding that there is a moral law and as such that there must be a moral law-giver. The argument has taken many different looks throughout the years but is easily understood the way it is posited by William Lane Craig. He writes, "If God does not exist, objective moral values and duties do not exist. Objective moral values and duties do exist. Therefore, God exists."[9]

The first premise of the argument shows that if morality is subjective, there is no need for a god to exist. This checks with all truth claims in the world. If there is no such thing as objective reality, then everything is subjective, and as such, this would work with morality. It is easy to acknowledge the truth of this first claim, even for those who do not believe in God. If there is no central singular guiding principle for the moral code, it can easily be seen that there is no moral code itself, thus making morals subjective. Some will say that we do not need this central figure to be God; however, it needs to be a figure that does not itself fall under these rules for morality. This must be a transcendent mind that sets these standards in place for all of mankind to follow. This transcendent character must also be present everywhere so that all of mankind can follow these rules and be powerful enough for these rules to apply to every human being that is alive or who will ever live. This is definitionally God, so this part of this premise is easily defended. This leads to premise two.

Premise two asserts that moral values and duties do exist. In looking at this premise, it is easily seen that there are objectively good and bad things. When someone claims that God (or His followers) is guilty of evil, this implies that there is an objective moral standard. We all intrinsically know that morals are objective. If morals are not objective, then Hitler was no less wrong in what he did than a philanthropist who gives all he has to charity. While this is an extreme case, it highlights the absurdity of stating that morals can be subjective, showing the need for an understanding of what is truth.

Once the two premises are understood to be true, the conclusion directly follows and thus is true if both premises are true. The point in expressing the moral argument as a full logical syllogism is to show that there will be few attacks against the premises, with the focus of opponents being against the conclusion. This is not proper argumentation, and as such, does not properly serve to disprove the argument itself. If one can see that each of the two premises is indeed true, it makes this statement necessarily true as well.

There are several points that are not made in this argument that those opposed to it will posit that it does say. The one opposition that is heard most often is that one does not have to believe in God to be moral. I do not disagree with this point, but this is not what the argument is claiming at all. This argument says nothing about belief in God being necessary for one to be moral; as a matter of fact, it shows that people are moral regardless of what they believe. This is an extremely weakened version of the argument that is presented, showing that a straw man is the only accepted way to stave off what the argument is claiming.

Cosmological Argument

The cosmological argument has been shifted many times throughout history but has been opposed to the possibility of an eternal universe. This is an argument of causes and shows that there can be no uncaused thing in the history of the universe. The argument is stated:

All things that begin to exist have a cause for their existence.
The universe began to exist.
Therefore, the universe has a cause for its existence.

Each of the premises is provable and exhibits the necessity of a causer. There have been many attacks on the cosmological argument, including Plato, who posited an eternal universe, yet many of the attacks recently have come against the conclusion even though it directly and logically follows from the two premises. Each of the two premises can be proven true, and as such, show that the conclusion is therefore true.

As one looks at all of the universe that can be studied, it is not shown that something can merely pop into existence. Fully formed trees do not just appear from nothing. Lawrence Krauss states that premise one is untrue due to elementary particles (such as quarks) are capable of coming into existence with no cause within a vacuum state. He based an entire book on refuting the first premise of this argument, but is he right? Does a universe come into existence like a quark, which will also spontaneously pop out of existence? These questions must be answered before one can continue within this argument.

David Albert, a professor of philosophy at Columbia University who holds a PhD in theoretical physics from Rockefeller University, believes Krauss thought to be in error. He states as much in his critique of Krauss' book A *Universe from Nothing* when he writes:

> Relativistic-quantum-field-theoretical vacuum states—
> no less than giraffes or refrigerators or solar systems—are
> particular arrangements of elementary physical stuff. The
> true relativistic-quantum-field-theoretical equivalent to
> there not being any physical stuff at all isn't this or that
> particular arrangement of the fields—what it is (obviously,
> and ineluctably, and on the contrary) is the simple
> absence of the fields! The fact that some arrangements of
> fields happen to correspond to the existence of particles
> and some don't is not a whit more mysterious than the
> fact that some of the possible arrangements of my fingers
> happen to correspond to the existence of a fist and some
> don't. And the fact that particles can pop in and out of
> existence, over time, as those fields rearrange themselves, is
> not a whit more mysterious than the fact that fists can pop
> in and out of existence, over time, as my fingers rearrange
> themselves. And none of these poppings—if you look at
> them aright—amount to anything even remotely in the
> neighborhood of a creation from nothing.[10]

So, even Krauss' theory of quarks popping into existence out of nothing does not seem to hold any ground when discussed amongst quantum scientists. The problem is that a vacuum is not nothing, and thus his problem is based on the mere definition that he uses in describing the event. Since even this refutation of the first premise fails, it can then be assumed that there are no uncaused incidents in the universe.

This leads us to the second premise of the argument. The thought of a beginningless universe is not only absurd in the mind of the thinker; it is a flat-out contradiction. There are no actual infinite sets, and as such, to attempt to make the universe one is laughable at best. Imagine a library with an infinite number of books. Half of the books are red, while the other half of the books are black. The question is, how many red books are in this library? The answer here is an infinite number. This would also mean that there would be an infinite number of black books. This thought experiment does not fully explain the lack of an actual infinite.

The other portion of this is that there would be no way to count in an infinite universe. If the universe were to be infinite, there would be no way to get to now, as there would be no point zero on the timeline. There would be no time for this to be possible to conform to. This stretches the imagination of even the toughest skeptic and requires a great deal of philosophical maneuvering just to get this point to be brought to the table for discussion. Since there are no actual infinite sets, then there must be a beginning. This means that the universe must have had a beginning.

Once this item has been determined, it logically follows that the universe has a cause for its beginning. When one drills down on that, this cannot be something that is found in the universe, which is a conglomeration of time, space, and matter. This means that the beginner must be timeless, spaceless, and immaterial. This beginner must also be powerful (it did create a universe) and personal (it created something). Once this has been determined, there would be a portrait of a divine Creator much like the one that is presented in the Bible. If this were the only evidence for the existence of God, it shows an excellent image, but this is merely the beginning of searching for the God of the Bible without ever opening the pages of one.

The Father, Almighty?

Once God has been pictured, there is a need to reconcile it with the God of the Bible to see if the pictures all fit together. There is a God, who created the universe from nothing (as proven by the spaceless, timeless, immaterial God), who has set forth morals for those whom He created (as the moral argument shows), who is (as the ontological argument shows), and who is a personal designer (teleological). This is the God that is portrayed throughout the entire corpus of Scripture and is called the Father by none less than Jesus. It is for this combination of reasons that one can come to rely on the biblical definition of God, as it has been logically shown in the preceding portion of this chapter.

Conclusion

As one looks into the question of who God is, it becomes easier to see that there are many false gospels in the world. This definition of God shows that atheism does not hold the weight that it purports to carry. This carries over to many of the atheist-like religions, such as Buddhism, Taoism, Daoism, and much of the new age movement. One must see God rightly to come to a full understanding of who God is, and as this book proceeds, the full picture of God will show that He is so much more than just the God of the philosophers, but that He is personal, loving, and that He has given the world one faith with which to live.

Chapter 3

Creator

Now that the picture of God has been established, this chapter will serve to further develop the understanding of who He is by providing a look at all of creation and providing reasons to believe that this is the creation that He intended from the dawn of time. There are many positions to take on creation, including day-age, day-gap, and literal traditions for the creation of the world. This text will take none of these positions outright because the Bible is quite frankly silent on this matter. This text will merely serve to show that the intelligence behind the design of the world and all life within it is immense and requires a designer. That there is sufficient reason for the Christian to believe that God created the world and all life within it and that this is the point of the entire body of Scripture. Without further ado, here are some of the arguments for creation by God, the Father Almighty.

Ex Nihilo

This phrase, as it is utilized within the context of beginnings, means "from nothing." This is the coming into being of everything from nothing. This is the primary concern for all of cosmology and is at the heart of the cosmological argument as it has been presented. The questions, even as it is answered by atheist scientists and philosophers, are how did nothing (what was in initial state) become something, and more importantly, how did life happen to come from non-life. The answers to these two questions show that there had to be intelligence behind the beginning and that this intelligence continues to guide the process. This process is called intelligent design, and while not a theory that will explicitly end with someone determining the God of the Bible, it shows that the god of philosophy, as proved in the first half of the last chapter, is more fully enveloped than is given credit for in the scientific arena.

When discussing *creatio ex nihilo*, it also becomes evident that this is the creation that is spoken of in the text of the Bible. This is lent from Genesis, Chapter 1, where, as God speaks, things are brought forth into existence. This is important to discuss when determining if the god that is presented through philosophy or the intelligent design movement is indeed the God of the Bible. As was shown through each of the philosophical arguments, a case can be made that the god that is expressed in the philosophical arguments has the same characteristics as God as He is presented throughout the text of the Bible. This chapter will focus on the intelligent design argument and how this can give Christian believers more pause to understand that the God of the Bible is true and how He is shown throughout the world, even in the fields of the physical sciences.

Intelligent Design

Stephen C. Meyer of the Discovery Institute, a leader in the intelligent design community, stated,

> In contrast (to evolution), the theory of intelligent design holds that there are tell-tale features of living systems and the universe that are best explained by an intelligent cause. The theory does not challenge the idea of evolution defined as change over time, or even common ancestry, but it does dispute Darwin's idea that the cause of biological change is wholly blind and undirected.[11]

This means that there is a need to understand where biological information comes from and to understand what is done with this information once it begins to exist. There are many in the atheist side that will attempt to merely explain away this information rather than dealing with the need that arises to fully deal with the data. When looking at this, there is a need to understand what some of these features are that have the appearance of design, and to look at what can be done to answer the design, to understand whether the hand of God is truly on these or if it is indeed all a matter of chance.

John Lennox, professor of mathematics at Oxford University, states that information is integral in understanding that not everything can be reduced. While irreducibly complex machines exist within the biological realm, he contends that "semiotics—signs like letters and numbers—cannot be explained in a purely reductionist fashion but require an appeal to the mind."[12] This essential to understanding how things are is irreducibly complex, and as such, is also immaterial. Information has no mass or matter, as was expressed by Norbert Weiner, the MIT mathematics professor who said, "Information is information, not matter or energy. No materialism which does not admit this can survive at the present day."[13] This means before material can even be explained, the words, symbols, or images used to explain them must exist. These words, symbols, and images then need an explanation as to how they came to be, and more importantly, how this information came to be understood. Materialist atheism cannot explain that away.

Semiotics does not seem to get the time that is needed to see that there is a definite problem with regards to abiogenesis. If there is information stored in the cell, and information requires creation, where did this information derive from in order to exist? This question creates a major issue for those who would state that the information just is, and even more so for those who attempt to state that this information could form randomly, with the order necessary for a cogent message coming from sheer disorder. Logically this takes the appearance of the watchmaker argument formulated by William Paley in his text *Natural Theology: or, Evidences of the Existence and Attributes of the Deity; Collected from the Appearances of Nature.* The difference between his argument and this one is that the argument is based on the evidence that is found solely in the realm of information.

While this is, by far, not the only argument for the existence of a Creator, it is one of the most powerful. It says that all information must come from a mind. DNA and RNA contain information. Therefore everything with DNA and RNA had to come from a mind. This shows that the information contained within these has to come from some mind that is beyond the intelligent replicators within the cell. This is the means by which one sees the need for a Creator in the sense of a being with a mind that is beyond all of that which has been created.

Now that the case has been presented from science for a Creator, attention needs to be turned to what the Bible has to say about a Creator God and who that is.

The Bible

The Bible has a great deal of information on the formation of the universe on whole as well as the formation of the earth. It begins in Genesis, Chapter 1, and continues through the creation of the new heavens and the new earth in the book of Revelation. This book will not discuss the debate between old-earth creation and new-earth creation, or even the evolution creation debate, as these are extremely nuanced topics, but will be satisfied by whether or not God made the heavens and the earth according to the Bible, since that is the detail that the Creed goes into when discussing this matter. This will be done through looking at the words as they are presented in the Word of God from Genesis through the end of the New Testament, seeing that God created everything, and this is why the historical interpretation of the Bible has largely been a creationist perspective.

Old Testament

The Hebrew word בָּרָא (*bara*) is translated in the Old Testament as "created," but literally means to be cut out of something or pared down. This would render Genesis 1:1 as "In the beginning God cut out the heavens and the earth." This still fits with God creating everything from nothing. This is why the translators render this as "created, " since this is the image that the author was giving of what God had done. He cut the heavens and the earth from the nothing that was present from the beginning. There are other words used within the creation narrative of Genesis, though, so this could just be someone utilizing this word out of context for the purpose of making the case for a particular brand of creationism.

The word is used seven times within the creation narrative and does seem to imply that the earth and all of its inhabitants were formed by the sovereign work of God. This word in its context seems to imply that this work was done by God alone and not through a process that took many years, though this is not necessarily the case when one looks at these efforts. The narrative remains that exactly, a narrative, and is not necessarily to be taken literally. This is not the only word that is used in the creation narrative to describe what was taking place at this time.

By the time a reader makes it from Genesis 1:1 through the rest of the narrative all the way to verse 7, there becomes a second word for what God is doing in the narrative. This second word is עָשָׂה (asah). Asah means to make or produce by labor. While it has other uses in the Hebrew language, this does tend to lean towards the use of making something through one's own efforts, regardless of where those efforts are seen. This means that there is a need to determine why the two words are used in the narrative and how the writer intended for these words to be taken. This word is used in a much more colloquial sense of the term to fashion. Is there a real difference between making and creating? This is what the question of these two words boils down to.

The words certainly overlap in meaning and usage, but there is certainly a reason for the use of each one when looking at the context of the matter. Frank Nelte writes on his website,

We can express the differences between these two Hebrew verbs as follows:

1) The Hebrew word for "create" implies bringing something new into existence by using only the Holy Spirit (the power of God) to do the creating.

2) The Hebrew word for "make" generally implies bringing something new into existence by working with, or making use of some things that were created previously. In other words, "making" generally presupposes that something used in the making process is already in existence before the new thing is "made."[14]

This shift in meaning certainly gives the reader pause to see what has been recorded as created (from nothing) and what has been made (from existing materials). This leads to a common error that is made, not just by those in theological circles, but also those who are using the Genesis creation account to dismiss the Bible, and that is that these words are used in different means and actually do compliment one another rather than giving one meaning. One shows that God created from nothing, while the other shows that He used materials that were made at the beginning point to fashion these things into other things which would yield their own type of creation. This does not answer, though, whether these days were the seven days thought of within the construct of the week on the world today.

Many will point to various theories that have become more popular within the last century to determine whether the days of creation are seven literal days. Many atheists will state that these are new ways to get around what the Bible says in an attempt to subterfuges the argument that has been made. There is a problem with their assertion that this is a new thought process, especially since there were published works on this thought long before science ever said that the world was billions of years old. This was initially presented by Augustine in his writing *On the Literal Interpretation of Genesis*, which was one of his final works. He looks at the writing of Genesis as a narrative rather than a timeline. As with any other narrative, there can be gaps in time in it that would allow for a much older earth than the one that is seen through a literal reading of the text. This view was accepted early in the history of the church by men such as Augustine, who said in this work,

> So for the sake of argument, let us suppose that these seven days, which in their stead constitute the week that whirls times and seasons along by its constant recurrence, in which one day is the whole circuit of the sun from sunrise to sunrise—that these seven represent those first seven in some fashion, though we must be in no doubt that they are not at all like them, but very, very dissimilar.[15]

Throughout his work on Genesis, Augustine cautions the reader against taking these days as days as one would understand them today, showing that this creation would have taken much longer than is thought of by those who demand a literal reading of seven days, showing that this discussion of how long were these days, or how they were constituted is not a new discussion, but one that has been taking place for the better part of the history of Christian thought.

None of this says one way or the other how "old" the earth is exactly, and as Augustine has illustrated, it was never intended to show that to the reader; it was merely designed to show that this was all the work of God. This is the key takeaway from the Old Testaments, and as such, serves as the way for each person to be able to grasp that the concept that God created the world and everything in it with the desire to continue His creation for years to come trickling on down the line until He would fashion each individual human being for His use. Since the Old Testament clearly teaches that God created the heavens and the earth, it is time to look at the New Testament's teachings regarding this very statement.

New Testament

The New Testament speaks volumes about creation and the creation narrative. From Jesus speaking about the individuals in the narrative (He refers to Adam and Eve, as does Paul) or from referring to the world as God's special creation. Each of these items will be seen as being what they taught as true, and as such, it is something that Christians definitely must believe in to be considered to believe in the orthodox set of beliefs. This is not to say that one must be a young earth creationist or an old earth creationist to be a Christian; they must merely believe in the creation of the universe by God at the beginning.

Jesus spoke of creation and the Genesis account through the flood on several occasions. The historian Luke takes the reader through the genealogy of Jesus all the way back to Adam in Luke. Jesus spoke of Noah in Matthew, Chapter 24, when discussing what the world would look like when He would return. This will come into play later in this book. The fact is that Jesus spoke of Noah as a person of history, the flood as a historical event, and the actions of the people to be historical. There are many who will state that Noah is a part of the creation narrative since from him comes the second wave of people from the offspring he took with him underway on the ark during the great flood. The flood has been questioned by many, both inside and outside of Christendom, but Jesus seems to be stating that this was a historical event. All of this being said, the first chapters of Genesis are spoken of in such a manner by Jesus as to believe that these were considered by God in the flesh to have actually happened.

Paul uses a great amount of creation discussion in his letters to the church at Rome, showing them why Jesus is celebrated as God. In Romans, Chapter 1, he discusses the proper creation of the world and what God intended of His creation. He uses a great deal of discussion of the perversions of society to show that they had strayed from the design of the creator. He continues this throughout the book discussing the implications of God's design and what that should mean to them as they begin to follow Him. In his letter to the church at Rome, Paul wrote,

> For the eagerly awaiting creation waits for the revealing of the sons and daughters of God. For the creation was subjected to futility, not willingly, but because of Him who subjected it, in hope that the creation itself also will be set free from its slavery to corruption into the freedom of the glory of the children of God.
>
> Romans 8:19–21

Here he is showing that this creation (from nothing) waits for the return of God and the glory of His return to be put upon them. He again uses similar wording regarding creation in many of his other letters, but all of it centers around one single Greek word, κτίσις (*ktisis*).

Κτίσις (*ktisis*) denotes a creation or creature. This word is used nineteen times in the New Testament writings, and as discussed above, is most prominent in Paul's letter to the Romans. Other writers would look at John, Chapter 1, to discuss the meaning of creation and how this came to be, but as a Jewish man attempting to show what God meant, Paul used the word that the Jewish believers would most likely have been accustomed to hearing in their own context. The second major word that was used to describe creation shows up in the book of John, and that is the word λόγος (logos).

In the context of the Greeks, this word would have meant a great deal more than is made of it in culture today. The Stoic philosophers had given a special meaning to this word that meant much more than had been made of this word previously. This word meant something akin to natural law. Chrysippus wrote, "If there is any common bond between gods and men, it is because both alike share in the Logos, which Logos is the natural law."[16] Likewise to the philosophers, the great philosopher-king, who was also a Stoic, Marcus Aurelius wrote, "...the Logos that extends through the whole of matter, and governs the universe for all eternity according to certain fixed periods."[17] This lays the groundwork for John's use of the word logos (henceforth used as Word). When John uses Word in his text, he is clearly showing the school of Stoics that Jesus was this natural law which was uncreated and, as such, was why there is something rather than nothing. This usage from John and the Stoics gives a solid foundational refutation of various cults, which state that this was clearly not what the Bible said. The Bible clearly states that the Word was God, and as that is established, this shows that John's use of Word meant much more to his desired audience than it would to those in the twenty-first century.

The use of logos by John was further described by Origen less than two centuries later when he wrote,

> But according to Celsus, God himself is the reason (Logos) for all things, while according to our view it is His Son of whom we say in philosophic language, "In the beginning was the Word, and the Word was with God, and the Word was God."[18]

This means that this understanding continued into the third century, though some of this understanding was propagated forth from Irenaeus in his work *Against Heresies*, where he equates the Word with the Aeons that were being celebrated by many Gnostic groups. This shows that the Word was thought of as the creative force behind everything, and as such, a concept took hold of those around the Gospel; those who sought to defend the Gospel were standing at the ready to use these things to define who God is and how His creation should be understood.

Conclusion

When looking at the evidence for a Creator, it seems as though science would side with the beginning creation of the universe. When looking at the biblical narratives, both the Old and New Testaments would side with the universe having been created. When looking at the evidence of the philosophies that were widely held at the time of the writing of the New Testament, this creation seems to have been what the writers were alluding to when they discussed the implications of the created world. These understandings have further been investigated through different thought experiments showing that the universe must have a beginning through the use of actual infinites, which have been shown time and again not to exist. When one realizes that the universe, as such, needs to have a beginning, philosophy again directs that the universe must have a cause for that beginning. This cause has been known by many names, Aeons, Logos, and wisdom, to name a few. The Bible clearly defines this as YHWH God, and in the New Testament, this attribute is applied to God's Word, who is also known better as Jesus Christ, the carpenter from Nazareth.

Chapter 4

Jesus Christ

While there is a great deal of information regarding the existence of Jesus written throughout the New Testament documents, there are many who will not accept these documents as proof for the existence of Jesus. Thus, for the sake of this chapter on whether or not Jesus existed, the focus will turn to the writings of historians who recorded the history of Jesus. Some of the focus of this will be on whether or not these historians can be counted on for the information that they provide on Jesus, as we weigh this against other claims made by these historians. While some of these writings will be used in later chapters, it is important to see that Jesus was indeed a human being who was active in the first century in the areas of Judea and Samaria. The evidence that will be included in this chapter has led such atheist scholars as Bart D. Ehrman, the sometimes agnostic, other times atheist scholar, to conclude in his discussion on Jesus mythicism and why it is wrong,

> Up to this stage in our quest to see if the historical Jesus actually existed, I have been mounting the positive argument, showing why the evidence is overwhelming that Jesus really did live as a Jewish teacher in Palestine and was crucified at the direction of the Roman governor Pontius Pilate.[19]

Josephus

The first name on the list is one that many know who are involved in the discussion on whether or not Jesus of Nazareth existed. His writings about Jesus will also be mentioned when discussing the Roman crucifixion of Jesus of Nazareth, but aside from that, this goes a long way to determining that Jesus was indeed a human being.

While a case can be made that some of the extant texts have been monkeyed with, scholars like Paul Maier have been able to conduct textual criticism on later editions of his writings and combine these with writings in other languages to best determine what was written by Josephus in the late first century. The importance of these two passages in Josephus cannot be undersold as he was a Jewish historian working with and arguably for the Roman Caesar.

The first passage of Josephus regarding Jesus is in reference to the death of James, the brother of Jesus. In book 20 of his *Antiquities of the Jews*, he wrote:

> Festus was now dead, and Albinus was but upon the road; so he assembled the sanhedrin of judges, and brought before them the brother of Jesus, who was called Christ, whose name was James, and some others; and when he had formed an accusation against them as breakers of the law, he delivered them to be stoned: but as for those who seemed the most equitable of the citizens, and such as were the most uneasy at the breach of the laws, they disliked what was done; they also sent to the king, desiring him to send to Ananus that he should act so no more, for that what he had already done was not to be justified; nay, some of them went also to meet Albinus, as he was upon his journey from Alexandria, and informed him that it was not lawful for Ananus to assemble a sanhedrin without his consent.[20]

While there may very well be Christian interpolation with regards to his being called the Christ, very little else of this passage can be called into question. This was a history of the Jewish people, and Christians were seen in the first century as a Jewish sect, even to those within Judaism. This seems to be a recorded incident in the book of

Acts, where there was yet another overlap. This occurs frequently between Josephus and the Bible, as these are the two primary texts for determining the history of first-century Palestine. This pales in comparison to the second reference, which brings in several of the characters from the biblical story of Jesus' crucifixion.

Here, the writer speaks of Pontius Pilate, the Sanhedrin, and Jesus Himself at the trial of Jesus. Josephus' writing on this event is subject to much debate since there has been a great deal of interpolation for this passage. Many historians have worked to determine what, if any, of this passage is authentic to the writings of Josephus, and the majority have determined that parts of this passage are original. The result of this text has been recreated using several key texts of Arabic descent, showing that this passage existed very early in the text's history. The revised text that these historians have come up with reads like this:

> At this time there was a wise man called Jesus, and his conduct was good, and he was known to be virtuous. Many people among the Jews and the other nations became his disciples. Pilate condemned him to be crucified and to die. But those who had become his disciples did not abandon his discipleship. They reported that he had appeared to them three days after his crucifixion and that he was alive. Accordingly, he was perhaps the Messiah, concerning whom the prophets have reported wonders. And the tribe of the Christians, so named after him, has not disappeared to this day.[21]

This reads with the omission of any claim that Jesus was the long-awaited Messiah, which had been added by later writers. Historically it is known that Josephus never came to believe in Jesus as the Messiah. Origen, who wrote a great amount against the heretic Celsus, would write in his own commentary on Matthew:

And to so great a reputation among the people for righteousness did this James rise, that Flavius Josephus, who wrote the Antiquities of the Jews in twenty books, when wishing to exhibit the cause why the people suffered so great misfortunes that even the temple was razed to the ground, said, that these things happened to them in accordance with the wrath of God in consequence of the things which they had dared to do against James the brother of Jesus who is called Christ.[22]

It can be seen here that Josephus' history is known by other writers very early in its distribution and that the history of Josephus as a person was known. Many in today's circle suppose that he might have become a Christian, but the truth regarding this can be found in the writings of the early church fathers. From a Jewish historian, we do see now that there are a couple of points that can be known about who Jesus was and how He died. These clues can start one on the path to determining who the historical Jesus is.

Tacitus

In his article "The Historical Jesus of Ancient Unbelief," Douglas Huffman states that,

Marcus Cornelius Tacitus (ca. AD 55–120) was a Roman historian who served as proconsul of Asia. In writing the section of his Annals (ca. AD 115) about Nero's reign, Tacitus acknowledges the simple (political) fact of Jesus' death when making reference to Christians without making any statement of belief.[23]

Tacitus, as he is commonly referred to, said a great deal about Jesus in the short statement he makes about his life, adding many of the same characters to the background of Jesus' life that Josephus had. According to history, Tacitus would have been given access to the minutes from the meetings of the emperor with various prefects called the Acta Senatus. Many of these documents would have been used in the creation of the *Annals* as well as the first book of his called *Histories*. While this is merely conjecture, as the official historian, he seems like a prime candidate to have been allowed access to these documents. This would have made his history reliable through the eyes of the Roman leadership and would have served as a way to ensure that the best history possible was being kept.

In AD 66, the year that Nero burned Rome to the ground, the Christians were sought out to be the scapegoats for this action. These Christians would be punished by Nero through a series of exquisite tortures and likely games at the Coliseum. It is at this point that Tacitus joins the conversation about these people, saying:

> To suppress this rumor, Nero fabricated scapegoats—and punished with every refinement the notoriously depraved Christians (as they were popularly called). The originator, Christ, had been executed in Tiberius' reign by the governor of Judea, Pontius Pilatus. But in spite of this temporary setback the deadly superstition had broken out afresh, not only in Judea (where the mischief had started) but even in Rome.[24]

This showed that the Empire was looking to fasten the guilt on someone, and who better than this upstart group of Jewish settlers who were causing some problems for him already. Thus is born the torture of the Christians in the Roman Empire and beyond. This leads to another Roman prefect who was attempting to determine how he should proceed with the punishing of Christians for their beliefs in a man referred to as Pliny the Younger.

Pliny the Younger

Pliny the Younger wrote a series of letters of inquiry and addresses to many individuals, cataloguing his questions and answers in a series of writings. He was a contemporary of Tacitus who would even write to Tacitus and serve as the chronicler for the eruption of Mount Vesuvius in which his uncle, who had adopted him, Pliny the Elder, had died. In his letters to and from various leaders, he asks questions and provides data for what he is seeing in various provinces that he was visiting or that he was mandated to go to for the gathering of information. One such chronicle from him to Trajan regarded a small sect of Jewish believers, which was outlawed. His questions were in how to deal with these criminals and to what ends he should hunt them down.

In part of his letter to Trajan, he writes concerning the practices of Christians, saying,

> That they were wont, on a stated day, to meet together
> before it was light, and to sing a hymn to Christ, as
> to a god, alternately; and to oblige themselves by a
> sacrament [or oath], not to do anything that was ill:
> but that they would commit no theft, or pilfering, or
> adultery; that they would not break their promises,
> or deny what was deposited with them, when it was
> required back again.[25]

His observation is just that, though. He is nowhere in this writing attempting to chronicle the day-to-day life of the Christians; he is merely asserting what he has either seen or what was reported to him. He adduces that he will not actively seek to try these individuals but will bring them to trial if necessary. Trajan agrees with his assessment.

The biggest thing that can be ascertained through Pliny's writing is that the early Christians (late first to early second century) worshipped Jesus as God. It can also be seen that Christians were indeed named for the Christ (Messiah) who they were committed to follow. There would be Christians who would recant from their faith (as both Pliny and Trajan imply), but these were few and far between. The steadfastness of those who were willing to suffer for Jesus was also noted by these two men. This brings us to a man who was awaiting his own execution at the hands of the Romans, Mara bar Serapion.

Mara Bar Serapion

Mara bar Serapion was a Syrian Stoic philosopher operating some time after AD 73 who was writing a letter to his son from a Roman prison as he was awaiting his own execution. While the text of his writing does not explicitly mention Jesus, he combines the destruction of major cities with the death of major people from these cities. He writes:

> What else can we say, when the wise are forcibly dragged off by tyrants, their wisdom is captured by insults, and their minds are oppressed and without defense? What advantage did the Athenians gain from murdering Socrates? Famine and plague came upon them as a punishment for their crime. What advantage did the men of Samos gain from burning Pythagoras? In a moment their land was covered with sand. What advantage did the Jews gain from executing their wise king? It was just after that their kingdom was abolished. God justly avenged these three wise men: the Athenians died of hunger; the Samians were overwhelmed by the sea and the Jews, desolate and driven from their own kingdom, live in complete dispersion. But Socrates is not dead, because of Plato; neither is Pythagoras, because of the statue of Juno; nor is the wise king, because of the "new law" he laid down.[26]

This does not serve to show the reader who the "wise king" was, but there can be inference based on the "new law" that Mara bar Serapion refers to that this would be Jesus. Some have stated that this was driven by a Christian and thus is not independent attestation from outside those who believe the Gospels. This does not appear to be true based on the lack of usage of "wise king" amongst those who were believers in Jesus. The destruction of the Jewish temple at the hands of the Romans appears to be the judgment he is referring to in his letter to his son and lends itself to the dating of after the year 73. The lack of naming Jesus is insignificant in that it would have been looked upon with scorn even mentioning the name and may have been seen in the eyes of his captors as words of insurrection.

Lucian

Lucian of Samosata was a Greek writer in the middle of the second century who was no friend of Christianity. He wrote on many varied topics, and many of his works survive to this day. One of his writings was *The Death of Peregrine*, in which he chronicles the death of a Christian convert who he does not speak well of, believing him to be a false convert praying on believers. He writes of how foolish these Christians were to accept this man into their midst and how their beliefs do not seem to match with what he knows of the world. All of these things combined show him to not be sympathetic to the Christian faith but do show many basic tenets of the faith that were taught in the first century. He writes:

> The Christians, you know, worship a man to this day—the distinguished personage who introduced their novel rites, and was crucified on that account... You see, these misguided creatures start with the general conviction that they are immortal for all time, which explains the contempt of death and voluntary self-devotion which are so common among them;

and then it was impressed on them by their original lawgiver that they are all brothers, from the moment that they are converted, and deny the gods of Greece, and worship the crucified sage, and live after his laws. All this they take quite on faith, with the result that they despise all worldly goods alike, regarding them merely as common property.[27]

These things combined show who Jesus was, that He was crucified, that the believers were not afraid of death, believed that the gods of Greece were false deities, and lived after the new laws that He had set forth. While this is not ironclad evidence by any stretch of the imagination, it does provide the historian with the works of Jesus and the early Christians to show who they were. The writings of Lucian are still around, as he was most likely extremely widely read. There were definitely writers who spoke of Jesus whose writings no longer exist, and these writings, recorded in the works of others, provide details regarding who this mystic was and why He was seen as important to those who were not Jewish in the first century.

Thallus

One such individual, Thallus, provides details of the darkness as well as the earthquake at the time of Jesus' crucifixion. This would be extremely useful information in showing that accounts of the Bible are true but are not seen as recorded by Thallus, but only through quotations by Sextus Julius Africanus in his work *History of the World*. Julius Africanus wrote,

On the whole world there was pressed a most fearful darkness; and the rocks were rent by an earthquake, and many places in Judea and other districts were thrown down. This darkness Thallus, in the third book of his *History*, calls, as appears to me without reason, an eclipse of the sun.[28]

His assertion against this opinion shows that this was a discussion in the first and second centuries, with people attempting to explain away the resurrection. Many have written regarding this since the time that the historian Thallus recorded that this was an eclipse, some stating exactly what he did, while many others have stated that this is not true as Julius Africanus did.

One such writer, Augustine, shows that this is not the case. In his seminal work *The City of God*, he wrote,

> For it is sufficiently demonstrated that this latter obscuration of the sun did not occur by the natural laws of the heavenly bodies, because it was then the Jewish Passover, which is held only at full moon, whereas natural eclipses of the sun happen only at the last quarter of the moon.[29]

This provides evidence that the early church did not believe in the sun's obscuring because they were some group of imbeciles who did not understand science, but because they understood how the natural world operated, they considered this to be an operation that was out of the ordinary, and as such should be recorded as one of the miracles associated with the life and ministry of Jesus of Nazareth.

The Bible

Now that it can be seen what the early world thought of Jesus, a first-century itinerant preacher, it is important to see what the writers of the Bible have to say about the life and ministry of Jesus, who was called the Christ. Throughout the New Testament, Jesus is referred to by many titles and names. He even refers to Himself as the "I AM," a name generally left for God alone to be called by. The writers clearly believed these things about Jesus, and many volumes have been written on the sayings of Jesus and whether or not He actually said them. The purpose of this is to see who the writers of the New Testament believed Jesus to have been and how this impacted their beliefs regarding the Jewish Messiah and those they would evangelize to in the years that followed the death of the One that the disciples called Christ.

The first portion to take a look at is Christ. This is the Greek word Χριστός (*Christos*) and is used in twenty-four of the books of the New Testament. In English, it is either translated as Christ or as Messiah. The Messiah was seen as "of the coming king whom the Jews expected to be the saviour of their nation and the author of their highest felicity."[30] This means that the Jewish people were looking for a coming king who would serve to take them out of bondage that they were in while under Roman rule. This is the definition that the disciples were working with when they were following Jesus. In Matthew, Chapter 16, Jesus was talking with His disciples, and He asked them about the Son of Man. They gave quite succinct answers. Then in verse 15, "He *said to them, 'But who do you yourselves say that I am?' Simon Peter answered, 'You are the Christ, the Son of the living God'" (Matthew 16:15–16). This shows that the disciples believed that Jesus was the coming Messiah, and is also why they did not believe that He was to be crucified, as they were looking for a leader on this earth.

The Messiah in Judaism is still looked upon as someone who will lead an earthly kingdom from the throne of David.[31] While the New Testament is clear that Jesus is the Christ, there are many in the religion of Judaism who would disagree with this concept. There were many prophecies regarding the Messiah that had to be fulfilled to usher in the kingdom. In the Old Testament, there were prophecies regarding many of the things that the Messiah was to go through, as well as who He would be in the flesh.

One such prophecy states that the Messiah would be of the tribe of Judah (Genesis 49:10). This prophecy is shown to be fulfilled through the tracing of His lineage in the book of Matthew.[32] In that same lineage, one can see that Jesus comes from the line of David, of whom God said, "Your house and your kingdom shall endure before Me forever; your throne shall be established forever" (2 Samuel 7:16). As if being born of the right line were not enough for a prophecy to be looked at as possible, the city of the birth of the Messiah would be Bethlehem (Micah 5:2), which was called the city of David. This is where Joseph and Mary made their way to when the census was taken as it is recorded in the Bible.

Many look at Jesus' triumphal entry as a really neat story, yet what is often missed is that His riding into Jerusalem on a donkey was the fulfillment of the prophecy of Zechariah regarding how the Messiah would arrive. Some give Jesus style points by saying that He set this up to be a fulfillment of prophecy, but then they have to explain away the first group of prophecies, since He could not have controlled where He was born, or even who His ancestors were if He were merely a man. With regards to things, He could not have possibly controlled; Daniel makes it clear that the Messiah would appear before the temple was destroyed after it was rebuilt. This means that the Messiah had to appear before the Romans destroyed the temple in the siege of Jerusalem in 70. As with His birth and life, there were prophecies regarding what type of death would befall the Messiah, but these will be covered more extensively in a later chapter.

All of this (New Testament writings combined with the prophecies) combines to show that Jesus was seen by His followers to be the Messiah. This is important when looking at this part of the Creed. The next part of this is to look at Jesus as the only Son of God.

One of the most famous verses of the Bible has been seen everywhere. It is present at sporting events, conferences, and even on the cover of Sports Illustrated (at least twice). During the 2009 National football championship where Tim Tebow painted John 3:16 under his eyes, this verse was googled 94 million times.[33] When he heard that number Tebow says, his first thought was, "How do 94 million people not know John 3:16?"[34] The question is, what is in John 3:16 that shows us exactly who Jesus is?

John 3:16 says, "For God so loved the world, that He gave His only Son, so that everyone who believes in Him will not perish, but have eternal life." The Greek word that is utilized there is υἱός (*huios*). This denotes a physical, familial relation of the Son to the Father. This is who Jesus is. He is the Son of God, but what does this actually mean about Him? To really see the implications of Jesus calling Himself the Son of God, one needs to look at how the people in the culture reacted after hearing Him refer to Himself as the Son of God.

In Matthew, Chapter 26, Jesus is in front of the Jewish authorities. The Bible says,

> But Jesus kept silent. And the high priest said to Him, "I place You under oath by the living God, to tell us whether You are the Christ, the Son of God." Jesus said to him, "You have said it yourself. But I tell you, from now on you will see the Son of Man sitting at the right hand of power, and coming on the clouds of heaven." Then the high priest tore his robes and said, "He has blasphemed! What further need do we have of witnesses? See, you have now heard the blasphemy; what do you think?" They answered, "He deserves death!"
>
> Matthew 26:63–66

This means that Jesus' statement was seen not as some figurative way of saying He was a creation of God but was, in effect, Him saying that He was on the same level as God. The leaders took this admission from Jesus to its logical conclusion and decided that it was time for them to be rid of this troublemaker. The charge He would face was insurrection against the Roman government (Jesus had called

Himself God, yet Caesar alone was God). While the Jews agreed that Caesar was not God, they needed to find some loophole with which to have Jesus charged. The real charge was blasphemy, but why was that the case?

To truly answer this question, one must search the Old Testament to see what the Jewish people believed about the Son of God title that Jesus was using. While Jewish scholars focus their attention on other places in the New Testament where the term Son of God is used, the problem arises when encountering the charge of blasphemy that extends from His use of the term in Matthew. This shows that there was a form of equality with God (not full equality) that was being stated by Jesus in His admission that He was the Son of God. Thus it can be seen that Jesus is presented in the New Testament as being the Son of God.

This brings about the final statement about Jesus in this line of the creed, where He is called Lord. There is a common question that has made the rounds throughout the centuries. It is generally posited by those of other religious beliefs because they are not looking at the meaning behind much of what Jesus has said throughout the New Testament; they look at His statements merely at face value. It goes like this, "Where did Jesus say, 'I am God, worship Me?'" This question brings up many interesting points of contention and serves as an excellent launchpad into the answer to the question of what does it mean to be Lord of all of creation and what did it mean when the Bible said that He was the Word in the flesh.

The Greek culture (Hellenism) and their beliefs in the gods play an essential role in the writing of the book of John, and this is seen from the very beginning of the book. In verse 1 of Chapter 1, John writes, "In the beginning was the Word, and the Word was with God, and the Word was God." The writer goes from there to explain that the Word became flesh. This Word, though, means something greater than what one would make of it in the English form. This is the Greek word λόγος (logos). The concept behind the logos in Greek culture goes far beyond what is seen in many other cultures. The early Greek philosopher Heraclitus is cited as having said,

> Of this Word's being forever do men prove to be uncomprehending, both before they hear and once they have heard it. For although all things happen according to this Word, they are like the unexperienced experiencing words and deeds such as I explain when I distinguish each thing according to its nature and show how it is.[35]

This is an early look at what the Logos was in a Greek context, as he wrote of it being eternal and that which set everything into order. This would not have been the understanding of the Jewish people of this Word, so it can also be seen through this that the gospel of John was mainly written to those who were Greek, if not in life, at the very least in their manner of thought. This serves as foundational knowledge to the concept of the Lordship of Jesus, so it is important to note.

There are several instances where Jesus is referred to as Lord in the Scriptures, with none as direct as the proclamation by Thomas, who had previously doubted the other disciples' accounts of the resurrection. Thomas' proclamation of Jesus as Lord and God is important to understanding what this all means; however, equally important in this exchange is Jesus' reply to his excited proclamation. John records this exchange in his twentieth chapter,

> Then He *said to Thomas, "Place your finger here, and see My hands; and take your hand and put it into My side; and do not continue in disbelief, but be a believer." Thomas answered and said to Him, "My Lord and my God!" Jesus *said to him, "Because you have seen Me, have you now believed? Blessed are they who did not see, and yet believed."
>
> John 20:27–29

Jesus is referred to as Lord and God in this one verse. If He were neither of these and He were to have been a good teacher only, He would have corrected His disciple. This creates a conundrum for those in Christian cults, such as the Jehovah's Witnesses, who claim that Jesus was merely a perfect man and not God since He gives accolades to Thomas for understanding who He is. Jesus is certainly happy that His disciple finally gets the point of His ministry. Through this, today's reader can finally see where Jesus refers to Himself as God since He tells Thomas that he has spoken rightly.

Conclusion

As Christians, belief in Jesus as the Messiah, the Son of God, and as He would be regarded, as God in the flesh is essential in the faith that has been passed down from the earliest of beliefs. This is why this statement is included in the Creed. It was seen as essential Christian doctrine in the first century and continues to be essential up to today. Any number of the early church fathers could be used to show that this has been the belief, as most of them used the phrase that Jesus was God or some form thereof, including Polycarp, Ignatius, Irenaeus, Clement of Alexandria, Tertullian, and Origen. The gist of what each of them said is encapsulated by Irenaeus when he wrote in his text *Against Heresies*,

> He received testimony from all that He was very man, and that He was very God, from the Father, from the Spirit, from angels, from the creation itself, from men, from apostate spirits and demons, from the enemy, and last of all, from death itself.[36]

Looking at what this church father stated, it is clear that those who had learned in the early church knew that Jesus was the Son of God, and as such, was God in the flesh.

Chapter 5

Christmas Story

There are various claims within the Christmas story that are coming not just from those who are opposed to Christianity but also from a large number of "Christians." Both of these groups say that Christmas is a pagan holiday. This parroting happens along the line with no one stopping to ask if it is actually true. The next portion of the Creed deals explicitly with two of the major claims of Christmas, so largely this chapter will deal with the major claims of Christmas, with an essential focus on the claim of Mary as a virgin (not a perpetual virgin) and the conception of Jesus through the Holy Spirit. Without further ado, is Christmas pagan? This chapter will not surprise you because the answer is absolutely not.

The Census

Before getting to the pagan roots of Christmas, it should be seen as to whether or not there was ever a census (around the time of Jesus' birth) that was called for by Roman rulership. This census would have to have occurred while Quirinius was in leadership in Syria and would have to have been assigned from the mouth of the caesar. If this point is not established, then there is no reason for Joseph to have taken his betrothed, Mary, to Bethlehem in the first place, and thus there was no reason for the child to have fulfilled the portions of the Old Testament which stated that the Messiah would have come from that city. Scouring through the annals of time has led to the realization that Emperor Augustus did indeed call for two censuses, and not the one that many have claimed. In his *Res Gestae Divi Agustini*, it is chronicled,

> Then a second time, acting alone, by virtue of the consular power, I completed the taking of the census, in the consulship of C. Censorinus and C. Asinius [8

BC]; at this lustrum 4,233,000 Roman citizens were recorded.[37]

This means that the census in 8 BC is likely the census that Joseph and Mary were responding to when they headed to Bethlehem. The question that remains is whether Quirinius was seen as a leader of some variety in Syria.

Quirinius is mentioned elsewhere in *Res Gestae* when Augustus writes, "A great crowd of people came together from all over Italy to my election, ... when Publius Sulpicius (Quirinius) and Gaius Valgius were consuls."[38] Through this lens, it is shown that Quirinius was seen as an important figure before he was the actual prefect of Rome to Syria. He was stationed periodically throughout the various portions of the Empire, and as such, could have been stationed in Syria during the time of this first census which would have made him familiar, not only with the process of the census but also with the area of Syria. This reconciles what Josephus had to say with regards to Quirinius being governor of Syria, especially since the word Luke used in his Gospel is ἡγεμονεύω. This word just means to be a leader. Luke also calls this the first census during his time as a leader. This would insist that there was a second census that would have been taken, matching what Augustus wrote. The next major objection to this is that Bethlehem was not a major city, if it was even a city at all.

Conception

Throughout history, people have said that the virgin birth is believed by Christians because they did not/do not believe in science. While there is a natural process coined parthenogenesis, this process has not been found to take place with humans or any of the mammalian species. Thus, scientifically speaking, this process is highly unlikely to have taken place. This comes back to the objection that humans cannot conceive without two parents and that those who believe this happened do not understand how science works.

This was Mary's objection when she was informed that she would have a child. "But Mary said to the angel, 'How will this be, since I am a virgin?'" (Luke 1:34) This shows that this was unexpected by Mary because she knew what the cause of babies was, and she had yet to be involved in such an act.

The angel quickly answers the young woman's question as Luke records saying to her, "The Holy Spirit will come upon you, and the power of the Most High will overshadow you; for that reason also the holy Child will be called the Son of God" (Luke 1:35). Not to be outdone, as if to assuage any difficulty that she would have with this, he informs her that her cousin Elizabeth, who is quite old, is also about to have a child. This serves as a way to draw attention to the fact that this was of God and not by human conventions that these things were happening. This was a miracle and one that she would not soon forget.

The problem one can run into with this is that there are those who say that miracles are not possible since they are in opposition to the natural order. This makes several key mistakes. The first is that these events are obviously abnormal, and this is why they are referred to as miracles and not what happens all of the time. This also assumes that there are no events that happen in ways that are not explainable by natural orders of events. This is problematic because it is an argument from ignorance. To say that something is not possible aside from a naturalistic explanation is to say that whatever is not understood by science will someday be able to be explained in a naturalistic way. This can be referred to as a "naturalism of the gaps" argument and should carry no more weight than the "God of the gaps" hypotheses.

In the second century, a Greek philosopher named Celsus, in an effort to undermine Christianity, discussed the virginity of Mary, giving the Roman soldier who had impregnated her a name, Panthera. While the work which contains this claim no longer exists, Origen would quote from this story in his book *Contra Celsus*, "When she was pregnant she was turned out of doors by the carpenter to whom she had been betrothed, as having been guilty of adultery, and that she bore a child to a certain soldier named Panthera."[39] Origen calls this statement out for what it was, a ploy to add legitimacy to the Jewish argument against Christianity. The evidence closest to the life of Jesus shows clearly that He was conceived by the Holy Spirit, and not because people in the first century did not understand how one became pregnant, but because this was what the angel had told Mary. This realization leads to a recognition of the virgin birth that was to take place in Bethlehem.

Bethlehem

If the Bible were to miss on something as simple as the birthplace of Jesus, why would one need to dig any deeper? The main problem, until recent times, with Bethlehem is that there were no records of this city existing, let alone it being a major city that would have been the hometown of a king, or even thought of as the probable place of the birth of the messianic figure of the Jewish tradition. These questions will be answered through the biblical text, which refers to Bethlehem as the place of Jesus' birth, and was even prophesied about before the Old Testament was closed out. This key event took place in Bethlehem, and the establishment of these key historical facts helps to set the baseline for the rest of what is read in the Christmas narrative as presented by the Gospel writers.

As with many other biblical locations, there are those who will deny that Bethlehem ever existed in any meaningful way. In 2016, a necropolis was discovered near the ancient town of Bethlehem, showing signs of this having been a fairly wealthy city with many artifacts dating to the Middle Bronze Age. One of the tombs discovered

> contained two Egyptian-like amulets, known as scarabs, which were mounted on rings made of bronze or gold... The scarabs date to the 13th dynasty

of Egypt (1802 BC to 1640 BC). One of the scarabs contains a series of circular decorations, while the other has swirling designs and what appears to be hieroglyphic writing.[40]

This sign of wealth and the early dating shows that this was likely an established city by the time of David, and while not the wealthiest city in the area was not absent of any people who were influential in history. Several centuries later, the king of Israel would come from this town and would change the narrative of the Jewish people for the rest of eternity.

Once Bethlehem can be seen as a city of some import in the region, it can be seen as less unreasonable that a leader could have been chosen from this city. In 1 Samuel, this is highlighted when this is where God is said to have sent Samuel.

> Now the Lord said to Samuel, "How long are you going to mourn for Saul, since I have rejected him from being king over Israel? Fill your horn with oil and go; I will send you to Jesse the Bethlehemite, because I have chosen a king for Myself among his sons."
>
> 1 Samuel 16:1

Samuel was not unconvinced of the need for him to go to Bethlehem, nor did he see it as untenable that God could have chosen the leader for His people from amongst this city. It is exhibited that Samuel was not blindly following but was using reasoning throughout this process when he is trying to discern which of Jesse's sons were to be the leader of Israel. It is at this time that he is told that David will be the next king.

This city would remain of some importance in Israel, as recent discoveries have shown through the discovery of a bulla. The discovery of this bulla in 2012 was the first discovery of the city of Bethlehem in the first temple period and provides evidence of economic activity in this region during this time.

> The stamp, also known as "fiscal bulla," was likely used to seal an administrative tax document, sent from Bethlehem to Jerusalem, the seat of Jewish power at the time. It was found as archaeologists sifted through mounds of dirt they had dug up in an excavation outside Jerusalem's Old City walls.[41]

This serves to show that this was not the "hole in the wall" town that had been previously purported by historians, showing instead that the economy was indeed moving through this city which would continue to be used throughout the rest of the Old Testament.

One key passage, which shows that the ruler who will reign for eternity, is Micah 5:2. This passage reads,

> But as for you, Bethlehem Ephrathah, Too little to be among the clans of Judah, From you One will come forth for Me to be ruler in Israel. His times of coming forth are from long ago, From the days of eternity.

> Micah 5:2

This means that the coming Messiah, according to Jewish prophecy, was to be born in Bethlehem, something which would not be under the control of this Messiah but would have to be met through the happenstances and free decisions of those who were in charge.

Two of the four Gospel writers, Matthew and Luke, record Jesus' birth as having happened in Bethlehem. It should come as no surprise to the reader that these are the only two writers that record this in such a manner, as Matthew was mostly concerned in his text with providing reasons for the Jewish people to believe that Jesus was the Messiah, and Luke was mostly concerned with accurately recording the history of the movement for his friend, Theophilus. These records do give clues as to when He was born, as was covered previously, as well as where He was born, giving the reader a developed image of what was happening at the time of Jesus' life. These accounts would not be the only accounts of Jesus' birth, as the church fathers would continue to carry this mantle.

Justin Martyr would provide one of the earliest narratives of the birth of Jesus that was written outside of the Gospels in his *Dialogue with Trypho*. He writes of this,

> But when the Child was born in Bethlehem, since Joseph could not find a lodging in that village, he took up his quarters in a certain cave near the village; and while they were there Mary brought forth the Christ and placed Him in a manger.[42]

This shows that there was, previous to his writing, a certain amount of tradition as to where Jesus was born. It can be seen through all of these documents various bedrock facts regarding Bethlehem. It can be seen that Bethlehem had a history as a city of import. This city was where David's family was from and continued to be a city of some import during the first temple period. This city would be the birthplace of the Messiah that was to come and would be where Jesus was born, with early attestation (around AD 150) given for the birth of Jesus in a cave in or near Bethlehem.

Virgin Birth

While some of the evidences in the Bible as well as the culture are the same for the virgin birth as it is for the conception of Jesus, it is necessary to show that this is a key tenet of Christianity that was fully developed by the advent of this creed. Often people will come against the virgin birth of Jesus for a variety of reasons, including those who say that this was a form of patriarchy, or that it was meant to be figurative, or even that Jesus was never born. These all miss great points that are made within the Scriptures, and this point will show that the two birth narratives were writing what was known to those who were with Jesus during His ministry. There have been arguments against the equation of the Hebrew term "alma" with the Greek term "parthenos" is incorrect, and as such, this is considered to be a faulty understanding of the Hebrew text by the New Testament writers, going so far as to state that they were operating from a faulty translation of the Hebrew texts. This can be shown by looking at this citation in its original context as it was written in Isaiah, and how Matthew understood this verse so far as his application for understanding the Jesus of Nazareth was born of a virgin.

When Isaiah writes, "Therefore the Lord Himself will give you a sign: Behold, the virgin will conceive and give birth to a son, and she will name Him Immanuel" (Isaiah 7:14), he is showing that the House of David will receive a sign, even though the leadership has refused to ask for one. There are those that think that this is a prophecy that is highlighted as having been fulfilled by Isaiah's own son to Ahaz; this can be looked at through the secondary fulfillment of the prophecy in Christ. The key word that is generally focused on in this text is the word עַלְמָה *almah*, which means literally young woman or maiden. This is used seven times in the Old Testament, and only four of these times is it translated as virgin, so it is not an emphatic statement that this is what his term means. If one looks at the full context of this verse, he is pointing to something that will be recognizable by large groups of people as a sign from God. To state that this is just a young woman giving birth is not to give a whole lot of a sign. If this were the sign, then this sign happens several times a day. Some will state that Matthew was reading the *Septuagint* (a Greek copy of the Jewish *Torah*). They will cite this as the reason Matthew translates the verse the way he does in his text, but as shown previously, this does not fit the full context of the Scripture.

In the first chapter of Matthew, he quotes Isaiah saying, "'Behold, the virgin will conceive and give birth to a Son, and they shall name Him Immanuel,' which translated means, 'God with us'" (Matthew 1:23). Matthew, in his text, uses the word παρθένος (*parthenos*), which means literally virgin. He took this as a literal virgin would give birth to a child. Since the passage in Isaiah was not used as a sign for the Messiah, it almost seems as though Matthew was looking at the Old Testament after the fact to see which passages one could conclude shows that the Messiah had come. One important facet of this to remember is that Matthew wrote his Gospel to a Jewish nation who would have laughed him off if he had misrepresented what was being taught in the synagogue if this were not the case. His gospel is instead seen as having a great deal of credence amongst the first-century Jewish population and is highly evidenced as having been written by exactly who is put as the author of the text. Matthew is writing that there was a virgin (Mary) who gave birth to a child (Jesus) without having had relations with her husband (Joseph). This was indeed a sign of the coming kingdom, just as Isaiah had prophesied about in his letter to the Jewish nation. The question remains, though, as to what the early church believed, with some people going so far as to claim that this was a later invention and should not be taught in the church today.

The problem with this view is that many of the church fathers directly stated that Jesus was considered to have been born of a virgin. Apart from what was written in Justin Martyr's discourse, this tenet of the faith can be found in Irenaeus, Polycarp, Tertullian, and Ignatius. In his letter to the Trallians, Ignatius writes,

> And God the Word was truly born of the Virgin, having clothed Himself with a body of like passions with our own. He who forms all men in the womb, was Himself really in the womb, and made for Himself a body of the seed of the Virgin, but without any intercourse of man.[43]

This means that Matthew is not writing this statement to show a birth to a virgin, but quite the opposite. He is showing that something that was written, that was not considered to be prophecy, turned out to indeed be prophetic with regards to the child that would bring peace to the world. In this way, the writings of the church fathers show themselves to help with a better understanding of orthodox beliefs today. Once the virgin birth is understood to be an actual event, it becomes necessary to look at the other events that took place during what is considered to be the Christmas narrative and see why these are not included within the early Christian creeds and what impact this has on the life of the believer today. One of the major events recorded in the biblical narrative is that the wise men came from the East. The question is, how real is this event?

What About the Wise Men?

The identity of the wise men is not a non-negotiable item in the faith of the Christian. Sure, since the Bible says that they were present, the Christian should believe it, but insofar as something that the true faith relies on, this is a deeply held moment in time that is often misunderstood as being part of the birth narrative of Jesus. The question that we should ask is not who came (this will get into that) but, moreover, when did they come? This is shown in the Bible and depicts something other than what is held as true in many mainline denominations today.

After being visited by the magi, Herod determines that he will attempt to rid the world of the newborn king, but he needs to know certain parameters before he can carry out his plan. Matthew writes,

> Then Herod secretly called for the magi and determined from them the exact time the star appeared. And he sent them to Bethlehem and said, "Go and search carefully for the Child; and when you have found Him, report to me, so that I too may

come and worship Him."

Matthew 2:7–8

When the wise men evaded Herod on their way out of the area, Herod then sent troops to Bethlehem to kill all of the children under the age of two. Why did he go after all children under the age of two? There are various clues to this in the Bible.

The first major clue to this is in the word that Matthew used in his describing the child. In the writing of the birth narrative in Luke, when the newborn child is mentioned by the angels to the shepherds in the field, Jesus is referred to as βρέφος (brephos). This would signify a baby, specifically one who was a newborn. The Greek word παιδίον (*paidion*) is used to denote a child, infant, or toddler. This would signify that some time had passed since Jesus had been born, though the Bible is silent with regards to how much time had passed since the birth. What it does say, though, is that Herod killed all children under the age of two. This would imply that the star had appeared in the sky around two years prior to the event. The next question that inevitably gets asked with regards to this is why this slaughter is not recorded anywhere else in history.

Macrobius gives some insight into why the slaughter of the Jewish children in the first century BC under Herod was not unthought of when he wrote,

> When it was heard that, as part of the slaughter of boys up to two years old, Herod, king of the Jews, had ordered his own son to be killed, he [the Emperor Augustus] remarked, "It is better to be Herod's pig than his son."[44]

When looking at the slaughter of children in a single town against the backdrop of everything else that Herod did during his reign, it becomes easy to see that this minor event would be overlooked by any who were seeing a need to record the events of his reign. This then would lead to the question of who these magi were that Herod trusted their counsel enough to commit to the slaughter of these children?

The magi appear to have been a group of individuals who studied a great amount of prophecies around the world and compared this to different astrological signs which would have guided their studies. This data matches a group of Zoroastrian scholars who would have been in the area of Baylon. This would have been the group that Daniel would have been part of during the exile that began during the ministry of Jeremiah and would begin to end at the time of Nehemiah. These magi would have studied these events and would have an entire community devoted to the findings of the group. The term utilized by the biblical writers for this group is (*magos*), which is a group of "magicians," the same group that Daniel would have been part of when he was in exile in Babylon. This group would have been familiar with the Hebrew prophecies, especially those which were made by Daniel himself. These would have been seen as important to them as this was the incoming king that Daniel speaks of when he writes about one as the Son of Man.

When discussing the magi, it is important to understand that these men were from a school that had studied apocalyptic writings from various sources and would have been familiar with the prophecies regarding this incoming king of the Jews. This being their forte would have made them apt to understand that they were going to welcome a child to the world. The keyword here is child. They would have understood that this was no longer a baby in a manger but would have been an infant or toddler based on their calculations of when the astrological event had occurred. While this is not agreed upon by any group of scholars as to what this event was or how old Jesus was when He showed up, it can most certainly be ascertained by looking at the different word usage between His dedication at the temple at eight days old and their arrival that some time had passed. It can also be seen by looking at Herod's response of killing all boys under two that He could have been up to two years of age. This shows that while it is certain that the wise men from the East did certainly come, it was most likely that this did not happen during the first days of the life of Jesus.

Conclusion

The Bible explicitly states that Jesus of Nazareth was conceived by the Holy Spirit and born of a virgin who was named Mary. This is shown through the writings of Matthew and Luke, the only two writers of gospels that cover the birth narrative in any depth. While Matthew does cite a text from the Old Testament that states that one was to be born of a "maiden," this was not generally believed to have been a messianic text at the time of the writing of the Gospels, so this would not have been needed to have been included unless there was something more to the story, such as it had indeed happened that way. The early church believed that Jesus was born of a virgin after having been conceived by the Holy Spirit. They also believed that the magi had witnessed an event in the night sky, which led them to the home of this new father and mother. This leads to an initial understanding of who Jesus is and what His mission on earth was, but it is by no means the end of the story, which truly only begins with the ending.

Chapter 6
Suffered

There are few facts that are as necessary to the truth of the biblical story as that of the death and burial of Jesus of Nazareth at the hands of Pontius Pilate. This story lays the entire groundwork for the resurrection. As has been previously shown, Jesus was a man who walked the earth. Another biblical figure whose historicity has been disparaged is that of Pontius Pilate. If He never existed, then a great deal of the story of Christianity is false and thus should be questioned, even by the most ardent of believers. Another key point that is often undersold within the community is whether or not Jesus actually died on the cross where He was hanged. If He never died, then the resurrection makes no sense as a hypothesis for the burgeoning religion. This chapter will seek to answer these two questions and show that the historical objections to the existence of Jesus of Nazareth's death at the hands of Romans who were acting on orders given by Pontius Pilate is not a work of fiction but is instead a historical event which has shown throughout time to be exactly as the Bible has shown it to have happened.

Pontius Pilate

When one looks through the corpus of information from the first two centuries regarding the crucifixion of Jesus, one character continually comes from the depths to show who the Roman Empire was to the occupants of Judea. This person is the prefect or procurator of Judea at the time, and someone who readers of the Bible will know, that is Pontius Pilate. Writers such as Tacitus provide an inroad to seeing who Pontius Pilate was and what his goal in crucifying Jesus would have been. In looking at Pontius Pilate as a historical character rather than some mythical "other," it can be seen who it is that is ordering the crucifixion to occur, as well as coming away with various historical details as to why he would have crucified a man who he found to be of no guilt. Whether one calls him a prefect or procurator is inconsequential as these terms historically appear to be used simultaneously. He is referred to in Roman writings as both a prefect and a procurator. The question that must be answered, though, is who Pontius Pilate was, and what can be known about this character that will lead to a better understanding of the circumstances behind the trial, death, and burial of Jesus of Nazareth in the context of first-century Judea.

The Gospels

The Gospel writers paint Pilate as the reluctant keeper of the peace with the Jewish leaders threatening a revolt if the teacher of this new religion is not put to death for blasphemy. He is eventually tried as a threat to the Roman government, but the question that remains with regards to Pontius Pilate in the Gospels is, "Who was he?" This will take place through the evaluation of several key passages of scripture to determine what is actually known of Pilate and how this matches with the historical accounts that are given with regards to what else had happened during his tenure as the prefect of Judea. When looking at the testimony of the writers of the four Gospels, there is a clear picture of the prefect and who he was. While each of the writers looks at different information, each shows a different aspect of the character of Pilate, no matter how subtle or absolutely villainous.

Matthew reveals that the governor would release a prisoner each year. While there are no sources outside of the Bible that establish this as having been an accepted practice, this does not seem to be out of the realm of possibility for Pilate, given the rocky start he had in the Judean province of Rome. When he had first come into Jerusalem, Pilate had waved the Roman standard all over the holy city. This caused a great deal of consternation amongst the leadership and would have required a great deal of flex for the prefect to have overcome this issue. Matthew uses the generic term for leader in Jerusalem in his use of governor, much the same way that Luke uses this term for Quirinius in Syria. This is likely due to the flux between the use of the terms prefect and procurator and is a sign of the ever-changing political and social landscape of first-century Rome. Some look at Pilate's desire to not put Jesus to death as a sign of his capitulating to the Jewish leaders but fail to understand that a second revolt during his tenure as governor would have spelled the end of his reign in the area and a loss of favor with Rome. Matthew provides hints as to who Pilate was and possibilities for why he did what he did, while Mark provides no extra data regarding Pilate. The bulk of the information comes from John.

John recorded the interactions with Pilate in several waves. In the first, he tells the Jewish leaders to judge Jesus according to their own laws. He knows that they will not be able to give Jesus a capital punishment and is apparently weighing his options to get them to give Him a lesser punishment. When the leaders refused to judge Him, Pilate understands that the capital punishment is all that would assuage their desire for punishment. Pilate then examines Jesus for himself. John records this in Chapter 18.

> Therefore Pilate entered the Praetorium again, and summoned Jesus and said to Him, "You are the King of the Jews?" Jesus answered, "Are you saying this on your own, or did others tell you about Me?" Pilate answered, "I am not a Jew, am I? Your own nation and the chief priests handed You over to me; what have You done?"
>
> John 18:33–35

Pilate would then hand down a corporal punishment to Jesus, having Him scourged for all to see. His desire was to see the bloodlust gone from the Jewish leaders. His calculation was incorrect. He then delivers Jesus to the people to decide His fate. The question he asks is whether Jesus or the renowned murderer Barrabus would be the one to receive capital punishment. He failed to understand that as the Jewish leaders went, so went the Jewish people. His plan again backfired as the Jewish people asked for Barrabas to be given over to the people. His hand was forced into giving Jesus the death sentence, against the wishes of Pilate and against the pleading of his wife.

Many paint the Pilate of the Bible as a sniveling puppet of the Jewish leaders, who is impotent, but as can be seen through the text, he was doing what was best for his own career and attempting to have nothing to do with the death of the carpenter turned rabbi. While he would fail in his own goal, the broader goal that he had in his dealings with the Jews of maintaining the peace in a tenuous situation had been accomplished. He had managed to keep the peace in troubled times, maintaining his control over the situation with regards to the Jews.

Tacitus

When looking at Tacitus' writing in his *Annals of Rome*, there was a call from the Jewish people which Pilate would have needed to heed in order to keep the peace which his actions had fractured to a certain extent. Pilate looked at the opportunity to put Jesus to death as a way to sway the favor of the populace towards being better citizens of Rome. Tacitus paints Christianity, a fledgling religion, as evil superstition and an upstart against Roman paganism. Tacitus' reference to Jesus gives us, the reader, a more complete picture of what was going on in the minds of Pilate. When he writes: through this passage, it can also be seen that Jesus was considered to be dangerous not just by the Jewish populace. In looking at the previous revolts against the Romans in Judea and how Pilate had handled these revolts, Tacitus wrote regarding the trial and death sentence of

Jesus when discussing Nero's own involvement with killing those who were followers after the fire that burned parts of Rome to the ground in his *Annals of Rome*. The passage that was previously referred to (see evidence for the life of Jesus) gives several clues into what this suffering looked like.

Key takeaways that can be gleaned from this passage include that there was an individual who Pilate saw that he realized he had to put to death, Christianity seemed to be in check for a while after Jesus' suffering, Christianity flourished throughout the Roman Empire, the early Christians were persecuted, and that they were willing to die for what they had seen. This passage does not state who was pushing for this death sentence, or why he agreed to it, just that this sentence was carried out on the one who was called the Christ (Messiah), who was brought before Pontius Pilate, and that coming out of his trial with Pilate was given the extreme penalty. Josephus fills much of the gap in, not in his writing about Jesus, which has been explored, but more so in the previous actions of Pilate.

Josephus

Josephus was careful in his handling of the history of the region of Judea. He was a Jewish man, which is one way that can be used to detect the interpolation in the text that is extant in his *Antiquities of the Jews*, which he wrote between AD 93 and 94. What is seen in his handling of Pilate is not much of a different picture than is given by the writers of the four Gospels. The revolt that could have occurred if Pilate had not crucified Jesus would not have been the first revolt during Pilate's tenure as the procurator in Judea. Josephus wrote,

> Now Pilate, the prefect of Judaea, when he brought
> his army from Caesarea and removed it to winter
> quarters in Jerusalem, took a bold step in subversion
> of the Jewish practices, by introducing into the city
> the busts of the emperor that were attached to the

military standards, for our law forbids the making of images.[45]

The people were highly offended that he would be willing to bring foreign gods into the Holy City, and this caused quite the fracture in the relationship between the ruler and his subjects. The Jews would request he remove the images, but he would continue to refuse to do so, until in Caesarea,

> When the Jews again engaged in supplication, at a pre-arranged signal he surrounded them with his soldiers and threatened to punish them at once with death if they did not put an end to their tumult and return to their own places.[46]

His cruelty and illegal trials would eventually be his demise, as he would be called back to Rome to stand trial for these very flaws in his character.

Eusebius

In his writings, Eusebius notes of Pilate's trial and the outcome. In his book *Ecclesiastical History*, Eusebius records Pilate's recall to Rome and his demise when he wrote,

> It is also worthy of note that in the reign of Gaius, whose times I have described, Pilate himself—he of the Savior's era—is reported to have fallen into such misfortune that he was forced to become his own executioner and to punish himself with his own hand. Divine justice, it seems, did not delay his punishment for long.[47]

He looked at the eventual death of Pilate (possibly suicide) as having been the judgment of God on Pilate. His history shows that Pilate did what he was commanded by the Empire, even to the point of his own death. While the merits of the hearsay presented by Eusebius are not the greatest, this passage cannot be overlooked as this shows that Pilate would do whatever was determined to be in the best interest of Rome at all times. It is seen that Pilate was a historical person, but there are still those who, until the Pilate stone was found, doubted his existence as a legend that was fabricated behind the fledgling Christian faith.

Archaeology

Until June of 1961, Pontius Pilate was relegated to sparse mentions through several writers, with none of them agreeing upon his actual title in the Empire. At that time, the first archaeological evidence for Pontius Pilate was discovered. Called the Pilate Stone, it is a carved limestone and is 82 cm by 65 cm. This stone has a simple declaration on it, which gives little information but does corroborate the information that is provided through historical texts. The stone's inscription reads:

[DIS AUGUSTI]S TIBERIÉUM
[...PONTI]US PILATUS
[...PRAEF]ECTUS IUDA[EA]E
[...FECIT D]E[DICAVIT][48]

This appearance of his name in Caesarea shows that he was in leadership while the Roman capital of Judea was there. It also provides the actual title of Pilate where it refers to him as a *praefectus* or prefect. The data that has been provided thus far has merely established the practices of Pontius Pilate while serving as prefect in Judea and serve as background data to the punishment that he doled out to Jesus, as he had previously done to many others.

Suffering

All four Gospels relate the story of Jesus' trial before Pontius Pilate. One of the punishments that is doled out to Jesus is that He is scourged. This was a barbaric act of whipping someone with a cat of nine tails with various metal and bone fragments intertwined into the whip itself. Within the scourging, the individual was generally stripped of all clothing that could impede the whipping. They would then be flogged from several angles to ensure that the one who received it was thoroughly beaten to the point of collapse or even death.[49] The details of the scourging of Jesus are sparse in the Bible, but what is known does not paint a picture that leaves much room for the hope of survival of the one who received the beating. There is no telling in these accounts whether the Romans were limited to the Jewish law of thirty-nine lashes, but it is stated that the soldiers were particularly cruel because they took a certain amount of enjoyment in knowing that Jesus had called Himself a king.

Died

The crucifixion of Jesus has been shown many times in various forms of art throughout the centuries. There are many aspects of this that have been challenged by various groups throughout time; the point here is to show that Jesus was crucified as the form of death penalty that He received. This means that there was a cross and a death that must be looked at. The Gospels record this event, though some have denied that this is the case. The first thing that should be looked at is whether or not the crucifixion was through the means that is believed by people throughout history. The second aspect is whether or not Jesus died as a result of His crucifixion.

Crucifixion

Seneca the Younger recounted the sight of seeing people crucified by saying that there were many forms of this. He wrote,

> I see crosses there, not just of one kind but made in
> many different ways: some have their victims with
> head down to the ground; some impale their private
> parts; others stretch out their arms on the gibbet.[50]

This means that there were varying styles of crucifixion that would have been conducted throughout the Roman Empire at any time. The question is whether Jesus would have been hung from a single pole (*crux simplex*), one shaped like a capital "T" (*crux commissa*), or one shaped like a lowercase "t" (*crux imissa*).

In 1857, a graffito was discovered with a drawing of a human body and a horse head nailed to a cross with a person worshiping at the foot of that cross; the inscription reads "ΑΛΕ ΞΑΜΕΝΟC CEBETE ΘΕΟΝ," which translates roughly to "Alexamenos worships [his] god."[51] It is believed that this is a picture of an early Christian worshiping Jesus. This would be tantamount to equating a worshiper of Jesus as somebody worshiping a donkey. In that this individual is described as worshiping his God, and he is at the foot of the cross, the belief is that this is Jesus on the cross. The Alexamenos inscription remains one of the first examples of a non-Christian describing Christians worshiping Jesus as God. As it dates to the second century (as a best assumption of the data), this provides the best view of which cross would have been utilized during the crucifixion of Jesus. The cross depicted is the one that has been common throughout the history of the church in that the *crux imissa* is depicted in the graffito.

Jesus Crucifixion

Regarding the crucifixion of Jesus, atheist scholar Bart Ehrman writes regarding Josephus' *Testimonium Falvinum*,

> The fact that he was opposed by the leaders of the
> Jewish people would no doubt have shown that he
> was not an upright Jew. And the fact that he was

condemned to crucifixion, the most horrific execution imaginable to a Roman audience, speaks for itself.[52]

Since Ehrman utilizes the pared-down version of this portion of Josephus' writing (which should be used by anyone looking at good historical data), there is no need to further delve into Josephus for determining if the crucifixion of Jesus truly happened. The data that is being utilized for this stance is where one must turn to see what is understood historically when discussing the crucifixion of Jesus. While a great deal of these have been looked at in the handling of whether or not Jesus existed, this data will be looked at again to determine whether the crucifixion took place.

Tacitus gives a good idea that Jesus was put to death under Pontius Pilate when he wrote:

> Christus, from whom the name had its origin, suffered the extreme penalty during the reign of Tiberius at the hands of one of our procurators, Pontius Pilatus, and a most mischievous superstition, thus checked for the moment, again broke out not only in Judæa, the first source of the evil, but even in Rome, where all things hideous and shameful from every part of the world find their centre and become popular.[53]

This passage gives the reader an idea as to what was going on and is presented by one who is hostile to the religion, thus, is most likely free of interpolation from later Christian scribes. The question that remains is whether or not this was crucifixion. This is handled by the understanding that the crucifixion was the worst form of capital punishment that was seen in the time of the Romans.

Death

The death of Jesus was accepted as a fact in the antiquities, so much so that His death is recorded, not only in the New Testament, but also in various other writers, Jewish, Greek, and even Roman. When the Roman writers speak of the death penalty, they speak as though the penalty that was inflicted never missed its mark. One first-century writer who spoke of Jesus was the philosopher Mara bar Serapion. In a letter to his son, Serapion, he speaks of the death of three great men, Socrates, Pythagoras, and the "wise king" of the Jews. He writes:

> What else can we say, when the wise are forcibly dragged off by tyrants, their wisdom is captured by insults, and their minds are oppressed and without defense? What advantage did the Athenians gain from murdering Socrates? Famine and plague came upon them as a punishment for their crime. What advantage did the men of Samos gain from burning Pythagoras? In a moment their land was covered with sand. What advantage did the Jews gain from executing their wise king? It was just after that their kingdom was abolished. God justly avenged these three wise men: the Athenians died of hunger; the Samians were overwhelmed by the sea and the Jews, desolate and driven from their own kingdom, live in complete dispersion. But Socrates is not dead, because of Plato; neither is Pythagoras, because of the statue of Juno; nor is the wise king, because of the "new law" he laid down.[54]

This early testimony seems to point to the wise king of the Jews that was killed by the tyrants of the Roman Empire. This testimony shows that this man was put to death, and given the timing fits very well with the person of Jesus who had a sign over His head on the cross that referred to Him as such. While contemporaries believed that Jesus was dead, it would be an article 1900 years later that would explain why Jesus died from a medical point of view. There was a great deal of uproar over the use of Scripture in a medical journal, but the journal only uses this to explain what the process was and how what was seen could have been so.

The Journal of the American Medical Association published a peer-reviewed journal article titled "On the Physical Death of Jesus Christ" by William Edwards, in which it discussed how Jesus would have died. This article points to the historicity of the crucifixion and how that death would have appeared to outsiders. In this article, Edwards chronicles the last day in the life of Jesus using the Gospel accounts to exhibit the conditions under which Jesus died. In the article, he discusses the wounds Jesus suffered through the scourging, His death by crucifixion, and even an account of the spearing Jesus' side. Throughout the article, the writer presents his findings regarding the practice of crucifixion in the manner which Jesus was forced to endure. The work also discusses the multiple medical conditions which would have led to the appearance of blood and water coming from Jesus' side when He was pierced by the spear. The conclusion that Edwards draws from his medical experience is the key factor in the paper. He writes:

> Thus, it remains unsettled whether Jesus died of cardiac rupture or of cardiorespiratory failure. However, the important feature may be not how he died but rather whether he died. Clearly, the weight of historical and medical evidence indicates that Jesus was dead before the wound to his side was inflicted and supports the traditional view that the spear, thrust between his right ribs, proba- bly perforated not only the right lung but also the pericardium and heart and thereby ensured his death. Accordingly, interpretations based on the assumption that Jesus did not die on the cross appear to be at odds with modern medical knowledge.[55]

The narrative of Jesus' life is not finished when Jesus breathed His last breath and exclaimed, "It is finished" (John 20:18). The Gospels continue to discuss the burial of Jesus in the tomb of a man named Joseph of Arimethea as well as His appearances in the flesh after He had been declared to have been dead.

Burial

This next point, the burial of Jesus, would be hard to explain if Jesus were not indeed dead. Joseph of Arimathea, a known individual amongst the Jewish leaders, claimed Jesus' body from the Romans. This means he would have had to have had a direct line to Pontius Pilate, as he is the only person who could have granted him access to the body once he was crucified. Throughout the Bible is described as a wealthy individual who was capable of having his own family tomb, which would mean that he would not be put to rest in the Jewish cemetery. This would allow for Jesus to receive a proper burial, not unheard of amongst those who were crucified by the Roman government. Some crucified individuals are known to have been laid to rest in family tombs.[56] This would have been the case if Joseph of Arimathea was willing to claim the body and lay him to rest.

It must be noted that the claiming and burial of the body had to be done before sundown since the festival was to start at sunset of that same day. Matthew records this event in Chapter 27, where he writes:

> Now when it was evening, a rich man from Arimathea came, named Joseph, who himself had also become a disciple of Jesus. This man went to Pilate and asked for the body of Jesus. Then Pilate ordered it to be given to him. And Joseph took the body and wrapped it in a clean linen cloth, and laid it in his own new tomb, which he had cut out in the rock; and he rolled a large stone against the entrance of the

tomb and went away.

Matthew 27:57–60

There are those who would assert that Joseph of Arimethea is a Christian invention, but his creation by the writers of the texts would make no sense due to the ability to easily refute the claims of his existence as a member of the Sanhedrin. It would be nonsensical to invent a leader of the Jewish believers in or around Jerusalem. Matthew, the writer to the Hebrew people, would not have included him in his apologetic text to the Jewish people if he did not exist, especially if the goal was to convert these people to Christianity. There is no reason to doubt the burial of Jesus as it is laid out in the Bible because there would have been no reason for the writers to create this event. They could have claimed a risen Messiah no matter where He was buried, so this shows a lack of necessity in the creation of this event.

Conclusion

While there are groups, such as Muslims, which will assert that Jesus did not die,[57] the historical data all shows that His death on the cross is as certain of an event as can be found in antiquity. With all of the data combined through history, through archeology, and through the scriptures, it can be seen Jesus suffered under Pontius Pilate, was crucified, died, and was buried. These become nearly indisputable facts, as Gerd Lüdemann stated in his book *The Resurrection of Christ: A Historical Inquiry* when he wrote, "Jesus' death as a consequence of crucifixion is indisputable."[58] Statements such as this one from an esteemed atheist scholar come across loud and clear in showing that the denial of Jesus' death at the hands of the Romans is ridiculous and flies in the face of honest historical inquiry. The point is as simple as Lüdemann puts it, that Jesus died as a result of His crucifixion at the hands of the Roman government. This is an integral step in affirming the next portion of the Apostles' Creed in that He had to have been dead for Him to be able to rise from the dead on the third day.

Chapter 7

He Is Risen

In 1 Corinthians, Chapter 15, Paul says that the entirety of the Christian faith rests on the resurrection of Jesus of Nazareth. He goes through an old Creed which states the fact behind the resurrection and how these facts should be used to build a case for who Jesus is. In his statements, Paul says that the resurrection of Jesus is of first importance. When he says this, he is saying that the resurrection is the most important portion of the Christian faith, so when we discuss the resurrection, we have to realize that this is the most important facet of all of Christianity. This is why so many books have been written on the topic of the resurrection. Scholars such as Sean McDowell, Mike Licona, and Gary Habermas have all written extensively on this topic, so this chapter will be a summation of the evidence for the resurrection of Jesus. Having already looked at the death of Jesus on the cross, it can be seen that this must be the fundamental starting place for a case for the resurrection, as it would be impossible for Jesus to have risen from the dead if He were not in fact dead in the first place. The next portion of the resurrection that must be considered is that the disciples believed that Jesus had appeared to them in bodily form. This means that the testimony that is written in the Bible is from eyewitnesses and does not match with the Bible, having been written a great deal of years after the death of Jesus. The complete commitment of the disciples to these facts cannot be ignored, as their testimony, which is found in the Gospels, shows throughout the writings of the New Testament.

The Creed

The creed that Paul gives in 1 Corinthians 15 says:

> For I handed down to you as of first importance what I also received, that Christ died for our sins according to the Scriptures, and that He was buried,

and that He was raised on the third day according to the Scriptures, and that He appeared to Cephas, then to the twelve. After that He appeared to more than five hundred brothers and sisters at one time, most of whom remain until now, but some have fallen asleep; then He appeared to James, then to all the apostles.

1 Corinthians 15:3–8

He concludes this by saying that Jesus appeared to him also. This creed is essential in understanding that the people listed authentically had a post-resurrection experience which they characterized as an appearance of Jesus. With the understanding that just because it is written down does not make it true, one has to look at the possibility of legend distorting the creed as it was written by Paul. Legends will generally form from people who are unknown to the teller of the story or the hearers of this story, will take place in a land that is far removed, and will have happened in the past, at a time that is unable to be accessed by those who are receiving the tale. The problem is that none of these traits are true of the creed that Paul is passing along here; most notably, he is writing down the story instead of speaking it to those in the church. The other problems that cause the formation of legends with regards to the people, places, and even the timeframe, do not fit the creed that Paul is passing along

People

Throughout the creed, Paul mentions several people by name and a couple of groups. The next step is to identify whether these people and groups identified this event individually as having happened. Seeing what each of these people believed with regard to the event that had taken place can show whether or not the claim that these people had seen something major actually happened or if there was just an attachment of names to the event. The first person mentioned is Peter, so he is the first person whose belief in the appearance of

Jesus should be observed with how this would impact his daily life and his ministry moving forward.

In the book of Acts, Peter is quoted as saying, "This Jesus God raised up again, to which we are all witnesses" (Acts 2:32). During his first sermon in Jerusalem, Peter declared that they had all seen the risen Jesus. This led to his boldness and his absolute belief that he was supposed to teach the words no matter what would happen to him. Clement shows the absolution of Peter's conviction that Jesus had appeared to him when he wrote:

> Through envy and jealousy the greatest and most righteous pillars [of the church] have been persecuted and put to death. Let us set before our eyes the illustrious apostles. Peter, through unrighteous envy, endured not one or two, but numerous labours; and when he had at length suffered martyrdom, departed to the place of glory due to him.[59]

As he states in this, it is important to see that Peter was certain of the resurrection of the body. This would be less clear if Peter were the only one of those who were present that showed a willingness to die for his faith. His stated desire to serve Jesus is stated by many other writers of the New Testament, including James, the brother of Jesus.

James plays a vital role in the ministry of Paul, but he is a far cry from the person that is presented in the Gospels. James, as well as Jesus' other brothers, was attempting to have Jesus go to Judea and Jerusalem, specifically during the Jewish Festival of the Booths, knowing that the Jewish leaders were seeking to kill Jesus (John 7:8–10). Something happened to make him believe in the person of Jesus. In 1 Corinthians 15:7, Paul states that James had seen the resurrected Christ. This would lead to his willingness to suffer for his belief in who his brother truly was. Eusebius and Josephus each record his death at the hands of the Jewish leaders. The problem is that these two records of his death appear to be completely contradictory to one another. This means that the problem is not whether or not James dies as a martyr, but how did he die? Josephus wrote in *Antiquities,*

> Festus was now dead, and Albinus was but upon the road; so he assembled the sanhedrin of judges, and brought before them the brother of Jesus, who was called Christ, whose name was James, and some others, [or, some of his companions]; and when he had formed an accusation against them as breakers of the law, he delivered them to be stoned.[60]

Eusebius adds that he was first tossed down from a pinnacle, with the final blow being from a club that was hurled at his head. Much like many supposed Bible contradictions, it is easily seen that these do not actually contradict but merely supplement one another. The question is, "Why did James willingly go to his death?"

Paul provides this answer for us in his creed by stating that the risen Jesus had appeared to James. This was one of the key factors listed in this creed, which took shape in the same city that James was the leader of the church. This would also explain why the leaders of the temple in Jerusalem would desire to have him put to death, so much so that they did not go through the necessary official channels to carry out the death penalty for this leader of the upstart sect of Judaism. His change of heart is not the only one amongst the list, as Paul added himself to an already existent creedal structure, showing that he was putting himself on the level of a Peter or even a James.

The change of Paul from Saul to the man who wrote thirteen letters of the New Testament is one that cannot be overstated in its importance. Paul describes his life as a Hebrew. He stated many times that he was a Jew of Jews from the tribe of Benjamin. F. F. Bruce describes the importance of this, stating, "Jerusalem, although formally allocated to Benjamin, actually formed an enclave between the two."[61] His parents' choice of the name of Saul even lends itself to the tribe as this was the first king of the Jewish people, who was a Benjamite. He would excel in his studies, becoming increasingly knowledgeable every year under his teacher Gamaliel, one of the best teachers in Jerusalem. He was brought up under the teachings of the Pharisees, which meant that he held to a strict standard of who God was considered to be. The first appearance of Saul in the New Testament is in Acts, Chapter 7, at the stoning of Stephen. This would set the stage for Saul breathing threats against the upstart group of followers of Jesus. He would travel from town to town, gathering up Christians for blasphemy and taking them to their death. The question that remains with Saul is, "How did this man so set against the followers of Jesus become one of them himself?"

Acts, Chapter 9, contains the answer to this question. Saul was on his way to Damascus when something happened. After describing what Saul was intending to do with the writs of arrest, the next thing shown is amazing and given account for several more times from the mouth of Saul. It says,

> Now as he was traveling, it happened that he was approaching Damascus, and suddenly a light from heaven flashed around him; and he fell to the ground and heard a voice saying to him, "Saul, Saul, why are you persecuting Me?" And he said, "Who are You, Lord?" And He said, "I am Jesus whom you are persecuting, but get up and enter the city, and it will be told to you what you must do."
>
> Acts 9:3–6

This was an appearance of Jesus to Paul. This would be the moment that would change the course of Saul's life and would lead him to take on the name of Paul. His own words numerous times show dismay at the former life and look forward to eternity with Christ. He points to this appearance as his call to be the apostle to the Gentile people, a call which he took seriously to his dying breath.

Clement also recorded the death of Paul when he wrote:

> Owing to envy, Paul also obtained the reward of patient endurance, after being seven times thrown into captivity, compelled to flee, and stoned. After preaching both in the east and west, he gained the illustrious reputation due to his faith, having taught righteousness to the whole world, and come to the extreme limit of the west, and suffered martyrdom under the prefects. Thus was he removed from the world, and went into the holy place, having proved himself a striking example of patience.[62]

Clement shows the manner in which Paul died was commensurate with his standing as a Roman citizen, thus leading to the understanding that Paul was beheaded, though this is less than necessary to understand that he had been killed for his faith.

While there are many people in this world who have willingly died for what they believed, these disciples are vastly different. These men were able to know whether what they had seen really happened. They were not led by belief but by what they claimed was knowledge. They had seen the risen Jesus, and this led them to willingly accept their death sentence rather than denying what they knew to be true. While this rare placement does not mean that they were telling the truth, it does lend itself to a certain amount of credence as evidence of what they actually had experienced.

Time and Place

This creed was popularized in the city of Jerusalem. This fact is important in understanding how legend could not have formed. The other major fact that plays into this scenario is that the creed is easily within five years of the events having taken place in Jerusalem. These two facts need to be understood to fully comprehend that this was not some fanciful delusion, as this delusion would have been quickly dismissed rather than thousands being baptized daily. While these facets of this cannot be set aside cavalierly, there is a need to place the creed here early for these statements to carry any weight. Gary Habermas asserts the importance of this creed on historical Christianity, saying,

> The importance of the creed in 1 Corinthians 15:3ff. can hardly be overestimated. No longer can it be charged that there is no demonstrable early, eyewitness testimony for the resurrection or for the other most important tenets of Christianity.[63]

In other words, this creed provides the data needed to exhibit the historicity of the resurrection.

Throughout modern scholarship, this is understood on many levels amongst even the most staunch of detractors to the Christian faith. Atheists such as Gerd Lüdemann and Richard Carrier have both understood this creed as being revealed to Paul by those in Jerusalem during his visit there. This would be required for Paul to be able to pass this on to the church in Corinth when he visited them in AD 51. This means that he would have received this creed around AD 37 or 38 when he visited Peter and James in Jerusalem. This means the creed existed in some form that was being passed around by this time, so the creed had to have been derived at some point prior to that. This back the creed up to somewhere between the death of Jesus and 35 or 36. This means that the creed formed somewhere between six months and two years after the death of Jesus. Lüdemann wrote in his book *What Really Happened to Jesus*:

> A fairly certain date can similarly be worked out for the conversion of Paul as well. The Acts of the Apostles credibly reports a stay of Paul in Corinth

when Gallio was there as governor of Achaia (Acts 18). Now this Gallio was in office in 51/52. (We know this from fragments of a letter of the emperor Claudius (4154), chiselled on stone, which were found in Delphi, the so-called "Gallio inscription.") If we calculate back from this date the intervals which Paul mentions in Galatians1:18 ("three years") and 2:1 ("fourteen years"), and add two years for travelling, the date of his conversion comes out at around 33. So we may state that the appearances mentioned in 1 Corinthians15:3–8 took place in the time between 30 and 33 CE (the fact of the appearances) because the appearance to Paul is the last in this list and is not to be dated later than 33 CE. The final form of its tradition (what the appearances were like) had not yet been fixed.[64]

As can be seen through all of this, the creed seen in 1 Corinthians, Chapter 15, began to show up in Jerusalem within the first months after the crucifixion, burial, and appearances of Jesus to people in and around Jerusalem. This is essential in understanding that these appearances were propagated as part of the Christian faith early in its formation and are not a later conjecture created by those who sought to gain power or to manipulate those who had no idea of what had happened at the time of Jesus.

Hypotheses

Since it can be seen that the disciples truly believed that they had seen the risen Jesus, there are many ways to attempt to run around the topic of how the disciples had seen the risen Jesus without the event having actually taken place. The major hypotheses that have taken shape throughout the years attempt to attack certain portions of the resurrection account while trying to preserve the historical backing behind the resurrection appearances due to the documentation having been written so close to the actual events. The three major conjectures that have taken shape in many ways throughout history are the swoon theory, the stolen body theory, the substitution theory, and most recently, the wrong tomb theory.

Swoon Theory

The swoon theory quite basically states that Jesus did not die on the cross so that the resurrection of Jesus is not brought into question, but that the physical death of Jesus is brought to the forefront. As exhibited previously, the death of Jesus is solidly placed as a historical event. This is not the only problem with the swoon theory, as this theory seeks to preserve the rest of the historicity of the Bible, and there are many reasons that the physical body would not have been able to perform many of the tasks held throughout the rest of the New Testament narratives post-resurrection, such as his traveling to Emmaus with two disciples. This seven-mile trip would have been difficult with the wounds on his feet. He would have been extremely disfigured by the flogging and subsequent crucifixion. This shows the ridiculousness of the swoon theory, especially more so in light of the evidence for the death of Jesus.

Stolen Body Theory

The stolen body theory is the oldest of the theories as Matthew records that this was what the Jewish leaders gave for the Roman soldiers who were guarding the tomb to state when asked how the body they were watching over had disappeared. Justin Martyr addressed that this hypothesis was in use by the Jewish populace in his *Dialogue with Trypho*, writing,

> As I said before you have sent chosen and ordained men throughout all the world to proclaim that a godless and lawless heresy had sprung from one

> Jesus, whom we crucified, but his disciples stole him
> by night from the tomb, where he was laid when
> unfastened from the cross, and now deceive men
> by asserting that he has risen from the dead and
> ascended to heaven.[65]

The biggest unanswered question that arises from this is, "Why would the disciples of Jesus willingly die for what they knew to be a lie?" This unanswered question leaves too much room for doubt that this happened, even though people like Richard Carrier believe that because this is even plausible, there is a need to fully account for this instance, regardless of what the rest of history states about this event.

Converse to what was being said regarding the resurrection of Jesus in the first and second centuries, many writers have come out in opposition of this within the first two centuries of Christian writing. Justin Martyr wrote how this was not true but was going around early. This hypothesis flies in the face of the actions of the disciples, as they would have been required to willingly die for what they knew to be a lie. While this means that the reader must attempt to psychoanalyze the disciples and their actions, the reader must take this into account when evaluating the evidence of the disciples' willingness to die for what they had seen. This puts this theory to rest, but it does not put an end to all of the hypotheses that are available to those who study the possibility of the resurrection being true.

Substitution Theory

There is a need to explain the death and subsequent appearance of Jesus to His disciples without denying the historical case for the resurrection of Jesus. Several other religions, including some Gnostic groups as well as some sects of Islam, have posited that there was a second body (twin) that was crucified in His stead. This stance makes a great deal of the information that was written later, giving it precedence over the earlier information from more reliable sources. The Qur'an says in Surah 4, verses 157 and 158,

> That they said (in boast), "We killed Christ Jesus the son of Mary, the Messenger of Allah, but they killed him not nor crucified him, but it was made to appear to them, and those who differ therein are full of doubts, with no (certain) knowledge, but only conjecture to follow, for of surety they killed him not: Nay, Allah raised him up to Himself; and Allah is Exalted in Power, Wise."[66]

This portion of the text is used by those who would discuss the possibility of a body double, but was not developed by Muhammad or his followers, but was adapted from early third century Gnostic source material, as were many of the beliefs of the earliest Muslim writers. In the book of *Thomas the Contender*, Jesus is quoted as saying, "It has been said that you are my twin and true companion."[67] In the later work of *The Acts of Thomas*, the resurrected Jesus appears "in the likeness of Thomas," the apostle, and is subsequently mistaken for Thomas by a king.[68] In contrast, there are other third-century (and beyond) texts that were developed by the Gnostic groups, with other people having been purported to have been crucified by the authorities in Jerusalem. The Acts of Thomas, Gospel of Thomas, and Infancy Gospel of Thomas were all heavily used by Muhammad and his followers as authoritative sources for the life and works of Jesus. This does provide the believer with a defense against this theory, leaving one less hypothesis for the non-believer to explain away the resurrection.

Wrong Tomb Theory

The wrong tomb theory states that the women and the disciples went to the wrong tomb and found that tomb empty. The problem with this theory begins with the fact that the women knew where the tomb was because they had been there previously. This also only accounts for the tomb being empty and does not account for the fact that the disciples believed that they had seen the risen Jesus. There are no early sources that account for the possibility that the disciples had gone to the wrong tomb. The lack of early source materials poses a major problem for those who posit this view today as this flies in the face of evidence that this tomb would have been known, not just to the disciples but to all in the area, as this was the tomb of a leader in the temple who was active at that time. Seeing as though all of these theories do not account for the early evidence that is presented in the Gospels, the testimony of eyewitnesses.

Testimony of the Witnesses

While there are scholars who will attempt to dissuade the readers of the testimony of the eyewitnesses being precisely that, and that there are other "gospels" that hold the same amount of weight as the four canonical gospels, this is simply a fabrication as to what the church has held since its genesis. The first-century writer Papias, in a document since lost to us, attempted to show which gospels were canonical in his writings, portions of which survive through Eusebius' *Church History*. His account was not the only one written, though, as he would be followed several years later by Ignatius. Ignatius was a student of Polycarp who had learned at the feet of John, one of the twelve disciples. His account of the formation of the gospels is found in the third book of *Against Heresies*. Here he recorded that in addition to the preaching that was being done around the known world:

> Matthew also issued a written Gospel among the Hebrews in their own dialect, while Peter and Paul were preaching at Rome, and laying the foundations of the Church. After their departure, Mark, the disciple and interpreter of Peter, did also hand down to us in writing what had been preached by Peter.

Luke also, the companion of Paul, recorded in a book the Gospel preached by him. Afterwards, John, the disciple of the Lord, who also had leaned upon His breast, did himself publish a Gospel during his residence at Ephesus in Asia.[69]

This gives the reader the distinct knowledge of who wrote the Gospels, in which order, and where the information was coming from for each. This text does not match with the level of current scholarship, which denotes Markan priority (that Mark was the first book), which will be further evaluated throughout this. To continue, the fact of the matter is that the list he provides the reader is in the order in which the texts are found within the canon of Scripture today.

Matthew

Before continuing on to determine which book was written first, it is best for the reader to understand some about those who wrote in the early church and whose quotations provide the basis for this determination. Papias is a key player in this as his testimony is the first to tie a specific disciple to the writing of these texts. Irenaeus, the disciple of Polycarp, wrote about Papias, saying, "And these things are borne witness to in writing by Papias, the hearer of John, and a companion of Polycarp, in his fourth book; for there were five books compiled by him."[70] This means that a disciple of John was the first to give clues to the writers of the New Testament Gospels. Papias wrote, "Matthew put together the oracles [of the Lord] in the Hebrew language, and each one interpreted them as best he could."[71]

Here it is easily seen that Papias understands who had written the gospel that now bears the name of Matthew. While there is discussion over what is meant by it having been in the Hebrew tongue, there are many who take this as a reference to the numerous textual references to the Old Testament that are present in the book of Matthew, which points to the group who Matthew was presenting his text as an apologetic to, the Jewish people. The text, as it is today, was clearly written in Greek, so his statement can be problematic yet is not unsolvable as it sits. This leaves the reader today with the book of Matthew, having been written by Matthew, the tax collector, as a defense of Jesus as the Messiah of the Old Testament to the Jewish people while Peter and Paul were in Rome,[72] was the first book of the New Testament that was written.

Mark

Aside from all that Papias stated regarding the writing of the book of Matthew, he gives more detail on the publication of the book of Mark. He says regarding this:

> And the presbyter said this. Mark having become the interpreter of Peter, wrote down accurately whatsoever he remembered. It was not, however, in exact order that he related the sayings or deeds of Christ. For he neither heard the Lord nor accompanied Him. But afterwards, as I said, he accompanied Peter, who accommodated his instructions to the necessities [of his hearers], but with no intention of giving a regular narrative of the Lord's sayings. Wherefore Mark made no mistake in thus writing some things as he remembered them. For of one thing he took special care, not to omit anything he had heard, and not to put anything fictitious into the statements.[73]

Here Papias notes the care that Mark took to add nothing to what Peter had been delivering in his speeches on who Jesus was. He also notes that Mark was not one of the disciples, nor was he a follower of Jesus during His earthly ministry. These are echoes of what was written by Irenaeus regarding the book of Mark, which he may also have received from Papias or even from Polycarp.

These two writers seem to answer the question of Markan priority, but the problem still exists in scholarship today. Who wrote first, Matthew or Mark? The answer seems to be Matthew before 65 and Mark shortly thereafter. Much of today's scholarship (liberal though it may be) is based on Markan priority due to the details of Mark (which invokes eyewitness testimony), the length of the discourses, the brevity of the book, and an apparent reliance on Mark by both Matthew and Luke. These issues do create somewhat of a quandary, but each is just as easily explained by the Matthean priority, with no additional explanation needed when looking at the writings of the early church. Regardless, the book of Mark as having been written early (sometime shortly after 65 or during a respite after Paul's first trial) as the testimony of an eyewitness (Peter) to the groups he was evangelizing to (those in Rome).

Luke

The book of Luke does not enjoy the extra amounts of early attestation for who wrote it, but the traditional view that was held by Irenaeus leaves little room to doubt who the writer was. To fully understand who wrote Luke, there is a need to look at the sequel, the book of Acts. Acts ends shy of the trial of Paul before Caesar and, as such, dates the end of the book at or near AD 61. Whether this is where the knowledge ended for Luke as he left on a journey, or this was the state that was known for Paul at the time of the writing is subject to conjecture, but it does show that this text was presented to Theophilus at or around AD 62 when Paul was said to have been released after his trial. This would place Luke at the beginning of this respite with Acts shortly thereafter. This leaves the writings of the church fathers intact and does begin to shed light on who these men were.

Luke was a physician. He was said to have been Paul's physician and traveling companion, which shows that Paul was suffering from the brutal conditions he had faced during his travels. His testimony of the Acts of Peter and Paul seems to have been carefully researched and shows the philosophy of these two men who were part of an upstart group that was attempting to bring a new sect of Judaism to the world. Paul desired to go into the whole world with the message of the cross and may have been able to proceed to Spain after his first trial in front of Caesar. This would have accomplished what he had written to the Romans. Luke was largely along for the ride with Paul and, as such, was able to see many of the sights that Paul had seen during his travels, and may have even been present at his trials. Luke seems to have been a careful historian as he includes many facts regarding the people and places that they had been, including necessary details that have assisted with the dating of the movements of Paul in the spreading of the early church.[74] This leaves only the Gospel of John in question, though the early writings of the church show that this question should be short-lived.

John

While many in the scholarly community do not accept the authority of the Gospel of John, there are several major early writings that show the authority of John in their writings. The Muratorian fragment, a small parchment from the third century, states that the apostle was one of the writers of the gospels. The writer said:

> The fourth of the Gospels is that of John, [one] of the disciples. To his fellow disciples and bishops, who had been urging him [to write], he said, "Fast with me from today to three days, and what will be revealed to each one let us tell it to one another." In the same night it was revealed to Andrew, [one] of the apostles, that John should write down all things in his own name while all of them should review it.[75]

This early attestation for the authority of John and his authorship of the fourth gospel stands as a foundational document for the canon of Scripture, showing that there was a need to know which books were accepted into the earliest of canons.

While Irenaeus also draws in the who with regards to the fourth gospel, much of his focus is on the why John wrote his testimony. The group called the Nicolaitans were spreading far and wide in their reach, and John had seen first hand how far-reaching they were. It was for this reason that he determined that he would set forth to write his gospel. Irenaeus stated:

> John, the disciple of the Lord, preaches this faith, and seeks, by the proclamation of the Gospel, to remove that error which by Cerinthus had been disseminated among men, and a long time previously by those termed Nicolaitans, who are an offset of that knowledge falsely so called, that he might confound them, and persuade them that there is but one God, who made all things by His Word.[76]

Irenaeus, having been one of the disciples of Polycarp, who was John's disciple, would have known why John wrote his testimony. This would have been essential in his learning. He would have certainly asked the "why" question. He provided the rest of the world with the answer to this question and was not the only person to discuss the authenticity of this gospel as having been written by an apostle.

Tertullian, a late second-century writer, states regarding the gospel of John,

> Of the apostles, therefore, John and Matthew first instil faith into us; while of apostolic men, Luke and Mark renew it afterwards. These all start with the same principles of the faith, so far as relates to the one only God the Creator and His Christ, how that

He was born of the Virgin, and came to fulfil the law and the prophets.[77]

Again, this places the apostle John as having written the fourth gospel. These texts all show that John, the apostle of Jesus, wrote the fourth gospel in response to the heresy of the Nicolaitans at the end of the first century while living in Ephesus.

The Gospels

The four gospels, as with the creed in 1 Corinthians, Chapter 15, are shown through the writings of the early church to have been written early in the life of the church by people who had first or second-hand knowledge of the activities of Jesus, including the fact that He was raised from the dead. The Gospels provide excellent background data for the resurrection and show what the disciples taught very early in the history of the church. The Gospels are foundational in understanding that the resurrection happened, as it was covered by the writers. The grave was empty, and the testimony of the apostles show that this was true.

The Resurrection

Christianity is set apart from other world religions through the resurrection of Jesus. While the evidence does not include a first-century non-Christian source citing the resurrection of Jesus as having happened, these small steps can be used in support of a case for the resurrection of Jesus. Looking at the importance of this resurrection and seeing who Jesus claimed to be, the resurrection gives the historian one valid answer to match all of the data available.

Chapter 8

Descended and Ascended

Once looking at the truth of the Gospels, it becomes easier to evaluate several of the portions of the creeds to determine where these primary beliefs were developed from and what they mean to believers today. There are many passages throughout Scripture that are more difficult to explain, but this does not make them less true. Once it has been determined that the Scriptures are indeed what they claim to be, it becomes necessary to look at the texts for what is truly being spoken and not to place a modern understanding on the text. When looking at these texts, they are best understood through the words of Jesus and the apostles and what was being spoken for others to understand. This keeps the reader from trying to place their own understanding on the text, instead relying on the text itself and determining what the writer truly meant within the confines of the text. Some of these texts are more difficult to understand than others, but nevertheless, it is the responsibility of the believer to attempt to understand these texts. These four portions of the creed are just as important to understand as the rest of the text but, for the first time, require a more complete understanding of the basics of the belief in Christianity.

Descended to the Dead

The first question that must be answered in this is what is meant in the original text. The Greek word for hell that is used here is κατώτατα (*katotata*). This word literally means to descend to the depths. A good explanation of this is found in Paul's letter to the church at Ephesus, where he wrote,

> Now this expression, "He ascended," what does it mean except that He also had descended into the lower parts of the earth? He who descended is

Himself also He who ascended far above all the heavens, so that He might fill all things.

Ephesians 4:9–10

This portion of Scripture shows that there was some contention as to what was meant by this by early believers, much as there is confusion as to why this appears to have been added later by Rufinus around 390 CE. For this, it is helpful to look at the body of the Scripture to see what Paul truly meant to gain a greater understanding of why this was added to the text.

Paul is explaining to the Ephesian believers that it was necessary for Christ to have been dead and in the tomb for the resurrection to have been of the importance that it was. As there are today, there were many who were stating that God could have just taken Jesus from the earth rather than having Him tortured and crucified. This descending to the lower parts of the earth shows that the grave was merely a stopping point for Jesus and that He would return to the earth before His final place. The psalmist also wrote of this saying, "For You will not abandon my soul to Sheol; Nor will You allow Your Holy One to undergo decay" (Psalm 16:10). This shows that Sheol is the place that Paul was talking about, as he would have been familiar with the texts of the Psalms and the intended meaning of this text from his time as a Pharisee.

The context of the word Sheol is king, where it is utilized throughout the Old Testament. The word is used sixty-five times in the Old Testament and refers to the unseen realm of the dead, the grave, the place of punishment for the wicked, or the place from where the righteous are saved. In the context of Psalm, Chapter 16, this word is being utilized as the grave. This means that Jesus actually went to the grave as a dead man. Though this was not the end of the story, the creed ensures that this part of the story is not forgotten in the midst of everything else. This is why His tomb being empty is of such importance and why there is a need to understand this. Yes, readers can accept the resurrection without this, but the fathers saw the importance of His body being gone from the tomb in which He was laid. The import of this word and its meaning must not be lost on the believer today.

This very issue is espoused by those who desire to show that the God of the Bible is a maniac or to prove a heretical form of Christianity (this is why it is important in the creed). The creed shows that there is a great deal of import placed on this key part for a reason. The most important facet of this is that the believer must know that Jesus was dead and put in a grave that He would rise from on the third day.

Ascended to Heaven

In Luke's second volume to Theophilus, the story of the ascension of Jesus to heaven is shown in the first chapter. He relays the story as follows:

> And after He had said these things, He was lifted up while they were looking on, and a cloud received Him out of their sight. And as they were gazing intently into the sky while He was going, behold, two men in white clothing stood beside them. They also said, "Men of Galilee, why do you stand looking into the sky? This Jesus, who has been taken up from you into heaven, will come in just the same way as you have watched Him go into heaven."
>
> Acts 1:9–11

From the beginning, Jesus made known that this world was not where He would consider to be home. There was no doubt that He at least considered Himself to be God's special agent that would bring about the end plan of God. This is the reason for the high number of references to the kingdom of heaven or kingdom of God throughout His talks. It should be of no surprise that His ascension into heaven made it into the pages of the text that was to be brought to those who would read of Him in the future. The two main points regarding this story are that He ascended and that this was Him going to heaven. These points require further amplification. What does it mean when the text says that He ascended? Was this a literal rising into the sky? What is heaven in this context? Is it an actual place? These questions will be handled in this section.

The Greek word for "ascend" that Jesus used in John, Chapter 20, is ἀναβαίνω (*anabaino*). This word means to move in an upward direction. Luke, Chapter 24, as well as Acts, Chapter 1, both exhibit that Jesus ascended into the sky as He was departing from His disciples. The intimacy of this event, as He was with His disciples, shows the drama that was attached to this event. This was the reason that His disciples were looking in an upward direction to see if they could follow along with His departure. This was an ascension in an upward direction, and the disciples were merely trying to follow the trajectory from their position on earth.

Jesus spoke of heaven many times as an actual place. One such example comes from the sixth chapter of John, where Jesus said,

> Therefore the Jews were grumbling about Him, because He said, "I am the bread that came down out of heaven." They were saying, "Is not this Jesus, the son of Joseph, whose father and mother we know? How does He now say, 'I have come down out of heaven'?"
>
> John 6:41–42

Jesus certainly speaks here of heaven as though it is a real place, and the Jewish leaders understood this as an actual place. If all of the teachers were teaching that heaven was an actual place, the disciples certainly understood it in the same way that the teachers did. Jesus left little doubt in His disciples' minds that heaven was a literal place, and not some figure of speech that was symbolic of paradise as some might be wont to suggest.

Through all of this, it can be seen that Jesus ascended to heaven and that the Jewish leaders understood what this meant to them. Heaven in the New Testament is called in Greek οὐρανός (*ouranos*). It is defined as the expanse of the sky or the dwelling place of God. The term is used over 270 times in the New Testament alone, showing the importance that Jesus placed on trying to live such that those who believe in Him and do the will of His Father will spend eternity in heaven. It can be seen that biblically Jesus ascended into heaven, showing that He is in the place where God is. He will be seated at the right hand of God.

Seated at the Right Hand of the Father

Jesus, being seated at the right hand of the Father, has been called specifically as the doctrine of the Session of Christ. Session derives from the Latin word "sessio," which means to be seated. This is regarded as an essential doctrine for who Jesus is and points to His divinity. If Jesus is seated on the throne, this points to His status as royalty in heaven. In his *The Book of Acts*, F. F. Bruce noted,

> The presence of Messiah at God's right hand means that for His people there was now a way of access to God more immediate and heart-satisfying than the obsolete temple ritual had ever been able to provide.[78]

While this is what the doctrine states, the believer must turn to God's Word and determine what the Bible says with regard to the seat of Christ in heaven.

In both Matthew and Mark, the words of Jesus to Caiphas, the high priest, are recorded on His way to Pilate. During his trial, Matthew records Jesus as saying, "You have said it yourself; nevertheless I tell you, hereafter you will see the Son of Man sitting at the right hand of

Power, and coming on the clouds of heaven" (Matthew 26:64). This was in response to the question of who Jesus thought He was. His response elicited a call of blasphemy and the tearing of the priestly garb. Through this, it can be understood that Jesus was claiming to be God in the flesh. The leaders of the church took this seriously and had Jesus bound and blindfolded while they took turns hitting Him, telling Him to prophesy who had hit Him. All of this for the claim that He would be seated at the right hand of power in heaven. This must have contained a deeper meaning than can be seen in today's language; otherwise, this would have been a massive overreaction.

The concept of the Son of Man, being seated at the right hand of the Father, evokes the picture that was seen by Daniel in one of the clear prophecies of the Messiah. Daniel was clear in stating that one as the Son of Man came to the Eternal God. This was seen as the Messiah, the one who was to come, and this was exactly who Jesus placed Himself on the same level. This was what the Jewish leaders were seeing in the claims of Jesus. They saw Him placing Himself on the same level as God. He had perpetrated a crime so grievous that the Old Testament called for the death penalty. He said that He was God. If it were not true, He should receive the death penalty under the Jewish laws, but as shown already, He was the God in the flesh. As this has shown itself to be the case biblically as well as historically, it is seen then that Jesus is on the throne to serve as the final judge.

Judge the Living and the Dead

There are several instances where Jesus places Himself as the judge of all, which also stands in line with Him stating that He is God in the flesh, as God is the judge of all that have ever lived. The Psalms are rife with the call for the judgment of God on the inhabitants of the earth. Psalm, Chapter 50, is a Psalm about such judgment as will come at the end of days. The psalmist wrote, "And the heavens declare His righteousness, For God Himself is judge" (Psalm 50:6).

The theme that is presented here is present throughout the entire Old Testament, showing that the Jewish people were to fear the Lord, as this was the beginning of wisdom for the people. God is presented as the judge of the nation of Israel throughout the prophets, bringing judgment in the flesh upon the people for their lack of love. This was clearly something that was a trait of God. Enter Jesus telling the people of Israel that He was to judge people at the end of time.

Jesus discusses the coming judgment as well as His role in this judgment. In Matthew, Chapter 25, His words are recorded where He said,

> But when the Son of Man comes in His glory, and all the angels with Him, then He will sit on His glorious throne. All the nations will be gathered before Him; and He will separate them from one another, as the shepherd separates the sheep from the goats; and He will put the sheep on His right, and the goats on the left.
>
> Matthew 25:31–33

He continues by stating that He would greet those on His right into the kingdom and would send those on His left into the outer darkness. This passage shows who Jesus thought He was and that there was a need for people to believe in His rule for them to be able to reach the eternal empire of heaven. This would not be the end of this declaration, as even those in the time of the apostles understood this to be what Jesus was saying and not mere hyperbole.

Paul, in his letters to the Romans and the Corinthians, exhibited to his readers that the throne of judgment belonged to Jesus. In Romans, Chapter 14, he refers to the judgment seat of God; however, in 2 Corinthians, Chapter 5, he writes, "For we must all appear before the judgment seat of Christ, so that each one may be recompensed for his deeds in the body, according to what he has done, whether good or bad" (2 Corinthians 5:9). This treats God and Christ as one and the same, with the judgment clearly coming from Jesus. Paul was not the last to write on this judgment seat which clearly shows Jesus as God.

In his *Epistle to the Ephesians*, Polycarp mirrored the words of the apostle Paul when he wrote,

> If then we entreat the Lord to forgive us, we ought also ourselves to forgive; for we are before the eyes of our Lord and God, and "we must all appear at the judgment-seat of Christ, and must every one give an account of himself."[79]

This shows that even one generation after the apostles that the judgment seat of Christ was still being taught as part of the case for Jesus being God. It also shows that it is believed that all will be judged by Him at the end of days. This combines to exhibit that it is clearly taught in scripture and by the church fathers that Jesus would judge the living and the dead; thus, all who have ever lived will be judged by Jesus on the merits of their faith in Christ.

Chapter 9

Holy Spirit

The Holy Spirit has been listed as many things throughout the course of Christian history, but none has been more striking than when He was called the forgotten God by Francis Chan. The third person of the triune God should be deemed as highly important in our society, especially amongst believers, yet there have been many who have decried His works, making the Holy Spirit out to be impotent in our time, saying that He does not work in the life of the believer the way that He did in the first century. The person of the Holy Spirit is important, but it also shows that there is a need to understand the divine traits of the Spirit. The divine traits of the Spirit are also important, but this shows that there is a need to understand the personal traits of the Holy Spirit. It cannot be missed that the Holy Spirit is indeed the third person of the triune God and, as such, has the traits of both the divine and the person of God.

Personal Traits

In all of the discussion of the Holy Spirit, the one thing that seems to get mentioned the most is that the Spirit is an impersonal force. This may be because this is a main teaching point for many cultic groups, and as such, separates them from the true Christian faith. The biggest proof for this is that the Spirit has many personal attributes that He is given throughout the Bible. There have been many volumes written on these attributes, so this will be a brief summation of the attributes to show His personal traits. Each of these shows who God is and how He is active in the life of the believer today. The Holy Spirit is deeply personal with a mind and will of His own, who can be grieved and resisted, yet who speaks, witnesses, and loves those who truly know Him. Each of these attributes shows the person of the Holy Spirit as He is presented throughout the text of Scripture and allows the believer to know better who God is. As these are presented in Scripture, the person of the Spirit becomes more clear to the believer of today.

Mind

In Romans, Chapter 8, Paul wrote,

> In the same way the Spirit also helps our weakness; for we do not know how to pray as we should, but the Spirit Himself intercedes for us with groanings too deep for words; and He who searches the hearts knows what the mind of the Spirit is, because He intercedes for the saints according to the will of God.
>
> Romans 8:26–27

With this verse, one must be careful not to overstate what is being said, as there are many misuses of this text for the purposes of promulgating bad doctrine. What this shows clearly is that the Spirit does have a mind that is separate from that of the Father and the Son. It is important to note that this passage shows that He is capable of cogent thought. As with all thought, this requires a certain amount of intelligence, which is another attribute that can be given to the Spirit. While these two attributes do not spell out that the Spirit is undoubtedly a person, it does lay a good foundation for establishing this fact.

In his commentary on Romans, Chapter 8, Matthew Henry wrote, "He knows what is in the mind of His Spirit in us."[80] This says that God knows what the Spirit is laying on the heart of the true believer in Him. This is because the Spirit is divine as the Father is divine. While the mind of the Spirit does layover into one of the divine natures He holds, it is the fact that He has a mind of His own that shows that the Spirit is working within the believer to accomplish what God desires of the believer. This is the reason that believers have such a high view of God and how the believer is able to act out what the will of God is.

The Spirit is constantly showing the believer more with regards to who God is, refreshing their mind. While the mind of the Spirit is closely related to the mind of the other persons of the Trinity, it is the will of the Spirit, which, while held close, shows His autonomy in many ways.

Will of the Spirit

While Paul was in the midst of discussing the spiritual gifts with the church at Corinth, Paul tells them who decides which gift will be given to each. He is clear in stating that these do not just "happen," but "one and the same Spirit works all these things, distributing to each one individually just as He wills" (1 Corinthians 12:11). This means that it is by the will of the Spirit that the gifts of the Spirit are given out. There are certain gifts that are seen as needs by God, who then freely gives. This is the subject of James 1:5 when he wrote that "if any of you lacks wisdom, let him ask of God, who gives to all generously and without reproach, and it will be given to him." This is one of the spiritual gifts that Paul was speaking of. This is accomplished by His will, but what does that word truly mean?

The Greek word that is utilized in this verse is βούλομαι (*boúlomai*), which means "electing or choosing between two or more things."[81] This means that the Spirit is able to select his own options from a variety of choices. This means that he must be able to make the determination from a set of desired outcomes without outside influences. He uses His mind to make decisions that are not determined by the other persons of the Trinity, and as such, He is free to act as He wills. His will can be resisted, and He can be grieved, showing that He is not some impersonal force.

Grieve the Spirit

Paul gives a great deal of emphasis to who the Spirit is and even goes so far as to caution believers in his letter to the church at Ephesus in how they act with regards to the Spirit. "Do not grieve the Holy Spirit of God, by whom you were sealed for the day of redemption"

(Ephesians 4:30). This means that a believer may choose to go against what the Spirit of God has given for them to do. This is the Spirit by whom believers are sealed in the faith and by whom we have been selected for the day of redemption. The believer is called to listen to what the Spirit guides him to do and follow.

While the text of the "Shepherd of Hermas" was written early in church history and for a time was considered canonical, it is still unknown who wrote the text. The writer said,

> Wherefore remove grief from you, and crush not the Holy Spirit which dwells in you, lest he entreat God against you, and he withdraw from you. For the Spirit of God which has been granted to us to dwell in this body does not endure grief nor straitness.[82]

The text states that the punishment for grieving the Holy Spirit is that God will withdraw from you, meaning that you will be outside of grace. It is made clear through this text that the Spirit can be grieved and should not be resisted.

Speak

The Spirit leads, has a will and a mind, and can be resisted. These may not make Him a person, but when combined with the fact that the Spirit speaks, it becomes much more difficult to deny His personhood. In Paul's first letter to Timothy, he wrote, "But the Spirit explicitly says that in later times some will fall away from the faith, paying attention to deceitful spirits and doctrines of demons" (1 Timothy 4:1). The Spirit is who gives the believer the picture of what is to come and how to deal with what is to come. It is up to the believer whether to hear what the Spirit is speaking to them and obey it or to brush it aside as though it were not the word of God coming to them. The Spirit of God still speaks, much like He did to the early church where this creed was derived.

Clement of Alexandria wrote of the speech of the Spirit, "The mouth of the Lord, the Holy Spirit, has spoken these things,"[83] as he was speaking to the heathen. He was exhorting them that they had heard the Word of God and that now was the time to follow what God had said to them through the Holy Spirit. He was making the point that has been made so many times throughout the course of human events that now is the time of salvation because tomorrow is not a given. He continues in this passage, saying that God was desiring for them to come to know who He is. That the Spirit had spoken to them so that they might not have to live in anguish and the torment of not knowing their Creator, but that they would come to love Him as the Spirit loved the one He was the witness to.

Witness

As with any court case in modern times, in the ancient times, witnesses were desired to establish guilt. Jewish law was such that two or more witnesses were required. In practical life, humans require evidence for anything that they will establish as a fact in their life; this includes religious decisions. The Spirit was sent to give people this knowledge and sent to be the witness that people desired so that they could know who God is. Jesus spoke of the Spirit coming as this witness for each person in John when he said,

> When the Helper comes, whom I will send to you from the Father, that is the Spirit of truth who proceeds from the Father, He will testify about Me, and you will testify also, because you have been with Me from the beginning.
>
> John 15:26–27

This witness to the truth of the Gospel message that Jesus came to deliver once for all should mean that those who hear the message should be transformed by the testimony of this witness.

As a witness to who God is, the Holy Spirit teaches believers. In the early church, there was a great deal of faith put into the Holy Spirit teaching those who were new to the faith. Origen writes concerning this, "We must therefore know that the Paraclete is the Holy Spirit, who teaches truths that cannot be uttered in words."[84] The Holy Spirit is the one who will guide believers in all knowledge of the truth, even in the absence of teachers within the church. For the believer, this means that the truth will be given by the Holy Spirit and that this teaching is beyond the comprehension of any earthly teacher. This also means that the Spirit will witness to who God is, the primary concern of any human being on earth. Some may liken this to a burning in the bosom; however, this truth will be verifiable because no witness was ever accepted in solitude.

Love

Many love songs are written in the world, but how many truly know what love is. Love, as written of in the Bible, is unconditional. It does not end. The Bible has chapters and even books dedicated to it, so it should come as no surprise that a personal Spirit would love human beings. Paul writes of this when asking for the prayers of the Roman believers when he wrote, "Now I urge you, brethren, by our Lord Jesus Christ and by the love of the Spirit, to strive together with me in your prayers to God for me" (Romans 15:30). The Spirit definitely loves believers. He loves them enough to desire (will) for them to hear Him when He speaks to them and to hope that they will follow what He calls them to do. The Spirit is a deeply loving person. Forces cannot love. Mechanisms cannot love. Persons can love. With the Spirit holding all of these personal traits as well as many others, it is easy to see Him as a person, but is He truly God?

Divine Traits

As important to understanding the third person of the triune God as seeing the personal attributes of the Spirit is that the Spirit is fully God as well. He is omnipotent, omniscient, and eternal, three major traits of God. As with the divinity of Jesus, though, some have stated that this was a later addition regarding the Holy Spirit and is not something that can be found in the Bible. This section will show that not only does the Bible, both Old and New Testaments, state that the Spirit is God, but also that the early church taught this before the word Trinity was ever being utilized. This will show that the Trinity has been an accepted concept within the church, not only since its early beginnings but also since the foundation of the text of the Bible.

Omniscient

The omniscience of the Holy Spirit is placed on full display throughout the book of Acts, but never so clearly as in Acts Chapter 5. The story speaks of Ananias and his wife, Sapphira. They sold a piece of land and brought some of the proceeds from the sale to the apostles for the church but stated that this was all that they had received for the land.

> But Peter said, "Ananias, why has Satan filled your heart to lie to the Holy Spirit and to keep back some of the price of the land? While it remained unsold, did it not remain your own? And after it was sold, was it not under your control? Why is it that you have conceived this deed in your heart? You have not lied to men but to God."
>
> Acts 5:3–4

Notice here that the Spirit knows what the land was sold for, and it was not the amount that was being spoken. Peter quickly calls this out. He also makes it clear that the land was Ananias' to do with as he pleased. He was under no compulsion to give all of the money he made for the purchase of the land. The only requirement that was given was that he was honest with Ananias. The second thing to note here is that Peter says that Ananias lied to the Spirit. He closes out with Ananias saying he had not lied to man but to God. This shows that the Spirit is considered by the writers of the New Testament to be God.

Throughout the Old Testament, the Spirit grants wisdom to the prophets to show the people of Israel what the consequences for their disobedience will be. In Ezekiel, he wrote, "As He spoke to me the Spirit entered me and set me on my feet; and I heard Him speaking to me" (Ezekiel 2:2). This shows that the Holy Spirit has knowledge of the future and can even state what is to come with a high level of fidelity. Those prophets who were speaking without the Spirit were said to not know God nor speak for Him. This once again shows that the Spirit of God is indeed considered by those in the Old Testament as God as well. Since the writers of both the Old and New Testaments believed that the omniscience of the Holy Spirit leads to His being known as God, it should be expected that the early church would believe this as well.

Towards the end of the second century, a little-known apologist was operating out of Athens, Greece, named Athenagoras. In his text *A Plea for Christians*, he makes many distinctions for right belief in God, especially for a right belief in the person and work of Jesus of Nazareth. In Chapter 10, he wrote about the work of the Holy Spirit, especially with regards to His work in the prophets. He wrote,

> The Holy Spirit Himself also, which operates in the prophets, we assert to be an effluence of God, flowing from Him, and returning back again like a beam of the sun. Who, then, would not be astonished to hear men who speak of God the Father, and of God the Son, and of the Holy Spirit, and who declare both their power in union and their distinction in order, called atheists?[85]

One must keep in mind that the charge of atheism was what would be levied against the early Christians since they refused to worship the gods of the Romans. It should also be noted that the Holy Spirit is who gives the knowledge to the prophets and refers to the power of God being with the Spirit. Seeing that the Holy Spirit has always been seen as being omniscient, the question must then turn to His omnipotence and whether this is a trait that He has.

Omnipotent

Mary was wondering how she could possibly get pregnant. After all, she had never been with a man. The angel answered her according to Luke, "The Holy Spirit will come upon you, and the power of the Most High will overshadow you; and for that reason the holy Child shall be called the Son of God" (Luke 1:35). The power of God, as it had come from the Holy Spirit, was to cause her to be pregnant. This shows that the Spirit of God is how the power of God can be shown to mankind. There is nothing recorded that is more powerful than someone that can bring something into being from nothing, and that is what the Spirit does time and again.

In the second verse of the Bible, the Holy Spirit is again seen as powerful in that He is present at the dawn of creation. The passage reads, "The earth was formless and void, and darkness was over the surface of the deep, and the Spirit of God was moving over the surface of the waters" (Genesis 1:2). Again the Godhead is present, and again, He is making something (in this instance, everything) from nothing. Those things which are spoken of as being unscientifically possible happen because of the awe-inspiring power of the Holy Spirit.

In the late third century, a writer by the name of Novatian wrote regarding the Trinity. When speaking of the Holy Spirit, he said,

> Who, working in us for eternity, can also produce our bodies at the resurrection of immortality, accustoming them to be associated in Himself with

heavenly power, and to be allied with the divine eternity of the Holy Spirit.[86]

This text shows that the power of the Spirit was considered to be the power of God. This should not be confused with the power of the Father. He also has the power to do and will as He pleases. The Son is also powerful in the creation and salvation narratives. The key is that each of the persons of the Trinity is powerful. The fact that the omnipotence of God is put on full display in the Spirit should come as no surprise since this is merely one of the attributes that are given to God throughout the corpus of Scripture. Now that the historical framework for the omnipotence and omniscience of the Holy Spirit have been resolved, even through the early church, it is time to turn to another omni- attribute of God, His omnipresence.

Omnipresent

God is ever-present. The Bible mentions this time after time. This is essential in knowing who God is. The psalmist says, "Where can I go from Your Spirit? Or where can I flee from Your presence? If I ascend to heaven, You are there; If I make my bed in Sheol, behold, You are there" (Psalm 139:7–8). This ensures the hearer that there is nowhere that one can run to get away from the Spirit. There is nothing that one can do to not be seen by the Spirit of God. He is everywhere at all times. He is the definition of omnipresent, according to this verse. The psalmist is talking about the covering up or hiding of sins. This is key to understanding this point. It even rolls into His knowledge of all situations. Ananias and Sapphira attempted to cover up their sin against the Spirit. They attempted to lie to Him.

He was not biting. He knew what had been done in secret, and He brought that knowledge to the light. This has to be taken seriously. When Peter asked Sapphira if the price they had given was the correct price, she answered in the affirmative. She was then struck dead just as her husband had been. The Spirit of God is with those who believe in Him. This means He is ever-present. This is shown throughout the Bible and even throughout the teachings of the church fathers.

Ignatius, while he was on his way to Rome, spoke through letters to seven churches and leaders that he had been in contact with throughout the area. In his letter to the church at Philadelphia, he wrote:

> Now, some suspected me of having spoken thus, as knowing beforehand the division caused by some among you. But He is my witness, for whose sake I am in bonds, that I got no intelligence from any man. But the Spirit proclaimed these words: Do nothing without the bishop; keep your bodies as the temples of God; love unity; avoid divisions; be the followers of Jesus Christ, even as He is of His Father.[87]

Here he highlights the fact that the Holy Spirit is capable of providing knowledge to a man, the way He was able to provide the same knowledge to the prophets and the apostles. He is showing that the knowledge of the Holy Spirit goes far beyond human boundaries and is capable of bringing to light that knowledge that is hidden, especially amongst His people. The only question that remains regarding the Spirit is whether or not He is eternal.

Eternal

Writers of the New Testament realized that since the Spirit was one of the persons of the triune God that this meant that He was eternal. It is captured vividly that this was the main way of thinking when the writer of Hebrews wrote regarding the sacrifice of Jesus. He wrote,

> For if the blood of goats and bulls and the ashes of a heifer sprinkling those who have been defiled sanctify for the cleansing of the flesh, how much more will

the blood of Christ, who through the eternal Spirit offered Himself without blemish to God, cleanse your conscience from dead works to serve the living God?

Hebrews 9:13–14

It does not get much more clear than explicitly calling the Spirit eternal. This means that the Spirit is without beginning and was present at the beginning. This echoes what can be seen when looking at Genesis 1:2 when the "Spirit of God hovered over the surface of the waters." This is essential to note. God created everything in unity. The Father, the Son, and the Holy Spirit were all present at creation.

Origen, who has had charges levied against him in the past varying from modalism to universalism, wrote extensively of who God is. In the first book of his, *De Principiis*, he wrote regarding the Holy Spirit,

But up to the present time we have been able to find no statement in holy Scripture in which the Holy Spirit could be said to be made or created, not even in the way in which we have shown above that the divine wisdom is spoken of by Solomon.[88]

This means he was searching for a way not to call the Holy Spirit eternal. He was seeking to put a notch in the rung of Him not being God, but he could not levy that charge against Him. Instead, he found that the Spirit was eternal. He was present for the creation of the world, and as such, he certainly believed that the Spirit was God.

Third Person

There are many who accuse Christians of being polytheistic due to their belief in the Trinity. This is not a new accusation, as many of the church fathers have had to discuss this very accusation. Tertullian, who coined the term "Trinity," was not immune to this. In his work *Against Praxeas*, he wrote:

That there are, however, two Gods or two Lords, is a statement which at no time proceeds out of our mouth: not as if it were untrue that the Father is God, and the Son is God, and the Holy Ghost is God, and each is God; but because in earlier times Two were actually spoken of as God, and two as Lord, that when Christ should come He might be both acknowledged as God and designated as Lord, being the Son of Him who is both God and Lord.[89]

As the evidence shows, the Trinity is true. The Holy Spirit is the third person of the Trinity as laid out in the pages of Scripture and in the writings of the early church. There is no doubt of who the Holy Spirit is or what He has done in the course of human events.

Chapter 10
Scary Words

During a speaking engagement at a church, a pastor came into the sanctuary and noted a copy of the Apostles' Creed hanging on the wall. He smiled at this, as he understood what the creed meant to the church, and felt almost as if he were among his kindred. As he read through the familiar words, he noticed a problem. One of the words had been blotted out and written over. Someone had changed the words to something nearly as old as the faith they preached. Why would someone do that? The answer was simple. The word "catholic" was an imposing figure looming large on the page. It was a terrifying word in the text. There were too many who did not know why that word, in particular, needed to be there. That word led to their confusion.

There are many words used in the church which can lead to confusion. These words are not meant to be scary and are not meant to drive a wedge between believers. As has been shown throughout this work, the creeds are to be used to give the true beliefs of those who are Christians. While these are not to be the only measure, they serve as the best magnifying glass for those who are of the faith. Too often, believers get into using "church words" to tell others about Christianity. Too often, those same believers get caught up on "church words" when looking at other sects of Christianity. The two words which are presented here are often misconstrued or misused, but when used rightly, they can give the believer a greater confidence in those they associate with when worshipping God. There are too many walls built for too many reasons, and as such, many of them need to be torn down and cast into the flames before they cause even more irrevocable damage to the Body of Christ.

Catholic Church

There are often two ways in which this word is taken, with both being off a little bit. Some will hold to the rigid definition that has been given to this word and will only use the capital "C" form of the word. This is a misnomer, as the word means so much more than just one church. Others will use this word too loosely and allow the meaning that is given to it to be too basic for the believer in that they take the meaning of the word as "universal." While this is indeed what the word means, it does not encapsulate why this word appears in the Apostles' Creed. The benefit of fully understanding the usage and context of this word within the early church is important. Often in today's church, there are those who will accuse others of heresy (departure from orthodox beliefs) with little to no backing behind the accusation.

Having a better understanding of the term catholic, how this understanding is meant to benefit the church at large, and what this understanding should do for each individual believer is important. This section will seek to give this understanding by providing a contextual understanding of the use of the word catholic in the creed, how the word was understood in the early church, and why the Bible speaks highly of worship in unity. These concepts are highly valuable in understanding what the creed means in the church today and why it should be implemented for each and every believer's benefit within the confines of the church. These concepts will come to light in this context and should be understood when proceeding through this portion of the text.

Context

To better understand the context of the word "catholic" in the Apostles' Creed, it is important to understand where the word derives from. The Greek word καθολικός (*katholikos*) means universal or general, but this word is not in the Bible, much like the word "trinity." In Acts 9:31, there is a statement regarding the growth of the church and the general peace. Luke wrote, "So the church throughout all Judea and Galilee and Samaria enjoyed peace, being built up; and going on in the fear of the Lord and in the comfort of the Holy Spirit, it continued to increase" (Acts 9:31). The words which formed together make Catholic are κατά (*kata*), which means throughout, and ὅλος (*holos*), which means complete. The first phrase of this verse, therefore, when discussing the church throughout all (*kata holos*), gives a picture of how there were separate bodies of those worshipping God, yet still one church. This unity of all of the churches is what this word is a picture of.

The church father Cyprian shows the extent of the seriousness of the doctrine of holding to one church. He expressed this in his seventy-third epistle, where he wrote,

> For it has been delivered to us, that there is one God, and one Christ, and one hope, and one faith, and one Church, and one baptism ordained only in the one Church, from which unity whosoever will depart must needs be found with heretics; and while he upholds them against the Church, he impugns the sacrament of the divine tradition.[90]

In other words, there are certain required beliefs in the church, and the believer must hold to these truths. There are certain beliefs that are up to interpretation but are not heretical, which should not cause one to walk away from the church. There are those who have left the church over non-essential doctrines; he regarded these people as following heretics. He refers to this single church as being a divine tradition, as was pointed out in the book of Acts, and throughout Paul's letters to the various churches in which he was providing counsel.

Rufinus, in his text on the creed, states the need for this is in refuting the heretical sects that had formed over the centuries. He said,

This is that holy Church which is without spot or wrinkle. For indeed many others have gathered together Churches, as Marcion, and Valentinus, and Ebion, and Manichæus, and Arius, and all the other heretics. But those Churches are not without spot or wrinkle of deceitfulness.[91]

This section must be included in the creed because there will be those who teach errant theology who will attempt to change the belief of the church as a whole. These sects show the absolute importance of knowing the creed and remaining as one body of believers.

Historical Use

Certain groups throughout history have taken words that were used in the past and reappropriated them in ways that they were not meant to be utilized. These pop up every day in the English language. The word that is being discussed here is obviously the word "catholic." This was never meant to be a denominational word, and the church was never meant to divide over words. This was meant to be a word that stated that everyone who held to the basic tenets of Christianity was part of the "one body" of believers, also known as the catholic church. Throughout the first two centuries of the church, this word did not mean what it has come to mean now. This section will seek to determine where the change in meaning happened and show that this change is preceded by something much greater than the meaning today.

Ignatius was the first person to use the word that is translated as catholic in text form. In his letter to the church at Smyrna, he wrote, "Wherever the bishop shall appear, there let the multitude [of the people] also be; even as, wherever Jesus Christ is, there is the catholic church."[92] This means that the believers should seek to have someone teaching who is capable of doing so, and the church should flock towards good leaders. He compares individuals flocking to good teachers (leaders) with the whole of the church flocking to Christ. This does not in any way seem to be an appeal to the "C" catholic church but appears to be universal in nature, as Schaff and Lightfoot explained in the previous section.

Shortly after the death of Ignatius, Polycarp, the great church father and another disciple of John, would be martyred in Smyrna. In the text titled *The Martyrdom of Polycarp*, the writer greeted the church at Smyrna, stating,

> The Church of God which sojourns at Smyrna, to the Church of God sojourning in Philomelium, and to all the congregations of the Holy and catholic church in every place: Mercy, peace, and love from God the Father, and our Lord Jesus Christ, be multiplied.[93]

Once again, this implies a certain unity of all those who believe in the basic tenets of the faith, no matter where they were located or who their teacher was. This again seems to fly in the face of what has been espoused by the Catholic Church in the modern era.

As a young man, Irenaeus had heard Polycarp teach what was written in the Scriptures. He formed a great deal of his theology early and put much of that on display in his text *Against Heresies*, where he wrote against the dangerous doctrines of the Gnostics. He established the rule of faith in the tenth chapter of the first book. With regard to what was necessary to know by those who are in the catholic church, he wrote:

> As I have already observed, the Church, having received this preaching and this faith, although scattered throughout the whole world, yet, as if occupying but one house, carefully preserves it. She also believes these points [of doctrine] just as if she had but one soul, and one and the same heart, and she proclaims them, and teaches them, and hands

them down, with perfect harmony, as if she possessed only one mouth.[94]

His teaching with these regards did not state that there was one denomination to rule them all; in fact, it seemed to state quite the opposite. He stated what everyone who professes faith in Christ is obligated to believe. Since there is one faith, the church is obligated to believe in the key points of doctrine and practice grace in those things which are not essential.

With all of these references to not just one church in a denominational sense, one would think that it had been this way for the entire course of history, but that is not so. This phrase was not tied to the Roman Catholic Church until around AD 350 when Cyril of Jerusalem, in his Lectures, tied this to the Catholic Church, stating that the Greeks were still waiting on a resurrection. He wrote of this,

> It is called Catholic then because it extends over all the world, from one end of the earth to the other; and because it teaches universally and completely one and all the doctrines which ought to come to men's knowledge, concerning things both visible and invisible, heavenly and earthly.[95]

While this seems to be the same universal church that previous writers had discussed, Phillip Schaff commented in his footnote:

> Bishop Lightfoot (Ignatius, ad Smyrnæos, viii.) traces the original and later senses of the word "Catholic" very fully. "In its earliest usages, therefore, as a fluctuating epithet of ἐκκλησία, 'catholic' means 'universal,' as opposed to 'individual,' 'particular.' In its later sense, as a fixed attribute, it implies orthodoxy as opposed to heresy, conformity as opposed to dissent." Commenting on this passage of Cyril, the

Bishop adds that "these two latter reasons, that it (the Church) is comprehensive in doctrine, and that it is universal in application, can only be regarded as secondary glosses."[96]

This shows that the scholarly opinion is that the definition of this word was changed later to better fit a doctrine that a certain group of believers had sought to show that other groups were outside the faith.

Unity through Diversity

Paul wrote a great deal about division in the church. None of his discussions were as prominent as what he had to say to the church in Corinth. This church seemed to have a penchant for dividing based on socioeconomic patterns in the area. Paul said that this was a bad plan and that they needed to figure out how to act as one body. He wrote:

> Now I exhort you, brethren, by the name of our Lord Jesus Christ, that you all agree and that there be no divisions among you, but that you be made complete in the same mind and in the same judgment. For I have been informed concerning you, my brethren, by Chloe's people, that there are quarrels among you. Now I mean this, that each one of you is saying, "I am of Paul," and "I of Apollos," and "I of Cephas," and "I of Christ."
>
> 1 Corinthians 1:10–12

The church today has to take heed to this. The church must ensure that the primary doctrines presented in the text of Scripture are what is being utilized to determine whether someone is in the faith.

Paul starts out by discussing that they should not be concerned about the pedigree of their faith. In the church today, one of the primary splits is over soteriology and the men that brought several differing opinions to the table with regards to how one is saved.

None of the three major positions (Calvinism, Arminianism, or Molinism) outright promote heresy in that they do not contradict with the main tenets of the faith outlined in the creed, so this is an in-house discussion and should not be a reason to break worship. This is a direct example of what the apostle Paul was bringing before the Corinthian church in this text, yet the church today seems to break fellowship over this matter on a daily basis. If this were the only reason that the church splits in today's society that Paul calls out in the first, that would be bad enough, but there is more.

The church in Rome seemed to be having some of the same problems as the church in Corinth. They could not seem to figure out how to get along well with one another. Paul wrote to them in his letter,

> One person regards one day above another, another regards every day alike. Each person must be fully convinced in his own mind. He who observes the day, observes it for the Lord, and he who eats, does so for the Lord, for he gives thanks to God; and he who eats not, for the Lord he does not eat, and gives thanks to God.
>
> Romans 14:5–6

Paul states throughout this chapter that there is a certain amount of liberty that Christians have in their worship of God, including the day of the week in which they choose to worship Him. This is another point of division in the church today, and Paul is clear that this should not be so. Paul gives a reason that these splits are happening, and this is a major sticking point for the church today. He says that the church divides as it does because there is a lack of love.

Jesus stated when asked what the greatest commandment is,

> "You shall love the Lord your God with all your heart, and with all your soul, and with all your mind.'

This is the great and foremost commandment. The
second is like it, 'You shall love your neighbor as
yourself.' On these two commandments depend the
whole Law and the Prophets."

Matthew 22:37–40

This feeds into the heart of the problem in the church today. Can
someone love God without loving those who are His? Can someone
love their neighbor yet want nothing to do with them? Has the
church forsaken the assembly of believers?

Communion of Saints

Some of the words in the creed have been used in more than
one way throughout the history of the church, and for that reason,
some of the words can lead to confusion. One such word that causes
confusion in the creed (almost as much as catholic) is communion.
Some feel as though this word, as presented in the creed, is the same
as the taking of the bread and the wine when conducting the Lord's
Supper. The problem is that this was not the concern that the framers
of the creed had in mind. Ignatius saw that there would be those who
would call out Christians for not worshipping on the Sabbath but
instead on the Lord's Day, which was considered the wrong day. He
countered this claim saying,

> If, therefore, those who were brought up in the
> ancient order of things have come to the possession
> of a new hope, no longer observing the Sabbath, but
> living in the observance of the Lord's Day, on which
> also our life has sprung up again by Him and by His
> death.[97]

This means that Christians were to be seen as congregating on the
day when new life had sprung forth, celebrating together that new
life. This communing together was referred to as the "communion

of the saints" and was seen as important enough of a tenet of faith that it was included in the basics, but the church seems to not know this.

Many in the church today would ignore the presence of believers of a different denomination in most contexts. In some instances, there are large chasms that must be handled before meetings can occur. Many in the world will look for another church until they find someone who has the exact same translation of the Bible, doctrines, or even skin tone as they do before settling into a church. This is not how the church is supposed to be acting on a daily basis. It is one body with different functions. There are many different ways to look at this within the context of the Bible, but the one key that must be recalled comes from Hebrews. The author writes,

> Let us hold fast the confession of our hope without wavering, for He who promised is faithful; and let us consider how to stimulate one another to love and good deeds, not forsaking our own assembling together, as is the habit of some, but encouraging one another; and all the more as you see the day drawing near.
>
> Hebrews 10:23–25

This command needs to be followed. The first part of this defines that the believer must have a confession for the hope in them. That is what the creed is all about. It is the rest of this that the communion of the saints is defined by.

Unity

Augustine is often misquoted as saying, "In essentials unity, in non-essentials liberty, in all things charity."[98] While this quote never proceeded out of his mouth, he wrote something much like it in his text *On Catechizing the Uninstructed.* He wrote,

In order that, although they vary in their capacities, they may nevertheless not lapse from the concord of charity, and inasmuch as it is especially in the fingers that there appears a certain kind of division, while nevertheless there is no separation from unity, this may be the explanation of the phrase.[99]

This speaks to the unity that is to exist in the church. Each body of believers may appear different to the outside world, but each body of believers should be another part of the same body of believers that extends the world over. There should be no ultimate separation between denominations. There should be no separation across social divides. There should be no separation based on which version of the Bible one reads. There should be no division based on which day of the week one worships God. These are worldly divisions that should not separate any two believers from one another. Yes, there will be cultural divides in the church based on these things, but it is the responsibility of each believer to ensure that they are not trying to create a fracture in the Body of Christ.

The Ending

The last three of the statements within the Creed refer to eschatology or the study of the last days. These statements are generally looked at through the lens of those who are involved in discussing when the end of days will be and what will happen at that time. The Bible allows for multiple viewpoints with regards to this, and these events were not seen by the early church as being particularly significant when discussing what was happening. Instead, the fathers stuck with looking at what was forgiveness of sins and how did that work. They discussed that the resurrection that was mentioned at the end of time was a bodily resurrection. The final point that they saw that needed to be discussed was the fact that life would be everlasting, especially with regards to those who were with God. Each of these was seen as important to the writers of this and as key doctrines that should be understood by the church at large; thus, these also need to be discussed as key doctrines for the church today.

The Forgiveness of Sins

To understand the forgiveness of sin, it is best to start with a proper biblical understanding of sin to set a groundwork for what is being claimed in this portion of the text. Sin in the Old Testament is חַטָּאת (hatta-at), which means "an offence (sometimes habitual sinfulness) and its penalty, occasion, sacrifice, or expiation; also (concretely) an offender." This word is used nearly three hundred times throughout the Old Testament, starting in Genesis, Chapter 4, and continuing through the writings of the prophets. This word was highly used in explaining what was happening to the Hebrew people, who were seen as the chosen people of God. They were suffering from their offence against God. In the New Testament, the Greek word used for sin is ἁμαρτία (hamartia). While the definition is expanded to include thoughts in the category of sins, the definition stayed largely untouched from what was being taught in the synagogues. In the first epistle he wrote, John talks a great deal about sin and what the rescue plan of God is for His people when he wrote,

> My little children, I am writing these things to you so that you may not sin. And if anyone sins, we have an Advocate with the Father, Jesus Christ the righteous; and He Himself is the propitiation for our sins; and not for ours only, but also for the sins of the whole world.
>
> 1 John 2:1–2

What John is saying in this passage is that Jesus came to die for the sins of the world (see also John 3:16–18) and that through His death, sin would be paid for, much as it had been through the sacrificial system provided to the Hebrew people.

Old Testament

Sin is discussed at length in the Old Testament, with many pictures of it as being a dirtiness that caused man to need washing. There are many pictures of the cleansing that was to come, but each of these systems would be held within covenants, each of which the people of Israel would break, leaving them as the idolatrous nation that God would cause to fall. There were periods of brightness for the people of Israel, though. David spoke of one of the times where the people knew there would be a forgiveness of sins. He wrote, "How blessed is he whose wrongdoing is forgiven, Whose sin is covered! How blessed is a person whose guilt the Lord does not take into account, And in whose spirit there is no deceit!" (Psalm 32:1–2) David is clearly not speaking of the Messiah figure in this because he speaks of the guilt of the individual that is not being counted against them. He speaks of their sin being covered by God. This is a picture of the forgiveness of sin that is shown through the resurrection of Jesus.

Isaiah gives a clear picture of how this would happen as he wrote about the messianic figure that was to come. He wrote, "All of us, like sheep, have gone astray, Each of us has turned to his own way; But the Lord has caused the wrongdoing of us all To fall on Him" (Isaiah 53:6). Each person has missed the mark and needs a plan for redemption. This plan would be presented for all to see on full display under the final covenant that God would make with His people. Forgiveness was put on full display for all to see at the cross of Jesus of Nazareth. This is shown throughout the writings of the New Testament.

New Testament

In his first epistle, John speaks of the sins of mankind a great deal. He ensured that even believers understood that they were not sinless when he wrote, "If we say that we have no sin, we are deceiving ourselves and the truth is not in us. If we confess our sins, He is faithful and righteous to forgive us our sins and to cleanse us from all unrighteousness" (1 John 1:8–9). The first portion of this passage touches on the Ten Commandments. Elsewhere it is written that all have sinned, so if one says that they have no sin, then they have called God a liar. This means that there is no truth in those that say that they are not sinners. The good news in this verse is that there is forgiveness for sin. John writes that God is faithful in forgiving sin. In other words, He can be trusted to forgive the sins of those who confess them to Him. This deletes the need for an intermediary between man and God in the form of a human. Jesus is that intermediary. The next statement says that God is right to forgive these sins. Unlike a bad judge who allows forgiveness, God serves as a good Judge, forgiving those who come to Him in faith.

Paul also spoke of forgiveness a great deal. This should come as no surprise since this was the impetus of his own salvation on the road to Damascus, breathing threats of death to those who were claiming to be followers of Jesus. There were a great number of things Paul had to be forgiven for, and as such, this played a great role in his writings. Paul closes out a portion of his letter to the church at Ephesus by stating, "Be kind to one another, tender-hearted, forgiving each other, just as God in Christ also has forgiven you" (Ephesians 4:32). He is showing the believers in Ephesus that God has forgiven them a great deal, and as such, they were to forgive those who had wronged them a great deal. Paul was speaking from knowledge that he had regarding his own salvation, knowing that he was even forgiven of the murders that were conducted at his behest. Paul was certain of God's forgiving of sins, and he passed this down for generations to come.

Fathers

Most of the church fathers believed that there was a need for confession of sins to take place for the people's sins to be forgiven. The issue that most modern believers would take with their statements is the absolution that would be given by the bishop (overseer) for these sins, who would receive the confession of the parishioners. This is seen as a Roman Catholic (or primary offshoot groups) rite that is unnecessary today. In the *Letter of Barnabas*, the writer stated,

> You shall judge righteously. You shall not make a schism, but you shall pacify those that contend by bringing them together. You shall confess your sins. You shall not go to prayer with an evil conscience. This is the way of light.[100]

This, the earliest non-Scriptural Christian writing, shows that the confession of sin is expected of the Christian before they come to God in prayer. This means that there is a logical step to confessing these sins to another, which would be someone who would be in a position of authority. This is not the way many Christians around the world would perceive this based on Jesus stating that He was the sole mediator for our sins.

Resurrection of the Body

There were two major sects of Judaism in the first century. As more evidence is discovered regarding other sects of Jewish believers in the first century, it has been seen that there were many other groups that were vying for the position of "God's chosen people" within the Jewish culture. There were indeed varying beliefs on which texts were considered sacred, who the prophets were, and even what was going on in the world. One distinction that is clearly seen between the two major groups, the Pharisees and the Sadducees, was with regards to the bodily resurrection of the dead at the end of days. Jesus spoke about the resurrection of the dead on several occasions, most notably when He raised Lazarus from the dead. Paul spoke about the Pharisees' belief in the resurrection of the dead at the end of days and cited this as the main point of contention between what he was teaching and what the Sadducees believed, thus causing a rift between the Jews, allowing him to go unnoticed. Through this, it can be seen that there was a Jewish belief in the bodily resurrection of the dead, something that is shown throughout the Old Testament that is again continued throughout the New Testament, and something that the fathers saw of enough import to continue writing about it throughout the entire course of church history. The question that remains for the believer today is whether or not the Scriptures show that there was to be a bodily resurrection of the dead and whether this was rightly placed in the creed.

Old Testament

Of the prophets who were studied heavily in the Jewish culture, few were looked to for an understanding of eschatology more than Daniel. The wisdom that he displayed throughout his exiles in Babylon and Persia was infamous not only among the Jewish people but most likely amongst the wise in Babylon, as discussed in the chapter on the birth of Jesus. Regarding eschatology, he wrote, "Many of those who sleep in the dust of the ground will awake, these to everlasting life, but the others to disgrace and everlasting contempt" (Daniel 12:2). Here he shows that the belief in the Jewish culture looks a lot like what was presented in the Gospels as well as in Paul's epistles as the beliefs of the Pharisees. He states that there will be those who are dead (asleep) who will wake up (rise) and go to a final place. Daniel spoke a great deal about the end of days, and while his writing is the clearest example that can be found in the Old Testament, this was not the only example in the Old Testament.

Isaiah was another prophet that spoke of the raising of the dead to life. While much of his work is prophetic in nature, there are many who state that his prophecies were too easily open to interpretation to be reliable; however, this is one prophecy that seems to be fairly straightforward. He wrote, "Their corpses will rise. You who lie in the dust, awake and shout for joy, For your dew is as the dew of the dawn, And the earth will give birth to the departed spirits" (Isaiah 26:19). This is a reply to the letdown that the Jewish people are experiencing, even though they have caused the letdown themselves. They were awaiting when things would improve for them as the people of God, and there was no end in sight. Isaiah was countering their thoughts on the dead staying dead and saying that there was no future hope, as he explained in verse 14 of the same chapter. He says that the dead will rise. He says that those who had rested in the dust would arise and shout for joy. This shows that there were definitely Jewish beliefs before the coming of Jesus that showed that there was a belief in the bodily resurrection of the dead, which leads to a need to see what was added to this belief in the New Testament.

New Testament

Jesus spent a great deal of time speaking about the world that is to come and what that world would look like. He spoke a great deal of the kingdom of heaven and how that will work for the believers in God. He also spoke about the bodies that believers would have. He said,

> Do not marvel at this; for an hour is coming, in which all who are in the tombs will hear His voice, and will come forth; those who did the good deeds to a resurrection of life, those who committed the evil deeds to a resurrection of judgment.
>
> John 5:28–29

This clear allusion to Daniel, Chapter 12, shows that Jesus was stating that He would usher in this time that was thought of as coming in the distant future. He was also stating His own divinity as He would be the One to conduct this judgment. This would be a resurrection of all, which shows that there is no annihilationist thinking in His statement. Those who were counted as righteous would be resurrected into everlasting life, while those who were counted as evil would be raised again to be judged. This shows that all will be raised again, but will there be a body?

Paul sought to answer this very question in his chapter on the resurrection. This is not a new question, as can be seen by the fact that Paul felt the need to address this very question. He wrote,

> So also is the resurrection of the dead. It is sown a perishable body, it is raised an imperishable body; it is sown in dishonor, it is raised in glory; it is sown in weakness, it is raised in power; it is sown a natural body, it is raised a spiritual body. If there is a natural body, there is also a spiritual body.
>
> 1 Corinthians 15:42–44

Paul uses the resurrection of Jesus and the fact that He had a material body (he ate, drank, walked, etc. after His resurrection) as a model for the fact that believers would have bodies in the resurrection, but that these bodies would be spiritual in nature. This shows that the earliest belief about the resurrection at the end of time would be bodily, though it is quite hazy with regards to what these new bodies would be like. This belief in resurrected bodies would carry over into the early church and would be espoused by many of the church fathers.

Church Fathers

Justin Martyr was one of the first writers that were prolific in the texts they had produced. His *Apologies* were instrumental in establishing a foundation for readers for centuries. Another of his works, *On the Resurrection*, deals directly with the question of what this resurrection will look like. He denied the physicalism that was rampant in the church at that time yet did not understate the fact that the raised body would indeed be a physical body. He wrote,

> If, then, neither of these [soul or body] is by itself a man, but that which is composed of the two together is called a man, and if God has called man to life and resurrection, he has called not a part, but the whole, which is the soul and the body.[101]

In other words, it would be a mistake to minimize individuals to just their soul or their body, but both must be accounted for since with either of these missing, the individual man would cease to be. Justin was born near the turn of the first century and was martyred around 165. He was a teacher and philosopher who came to Christ as a Samaritan. This shows that people were leaving their own religious institutions and embracing Christianity very early in the development of Christianity. It also shows that philosophically Christianity has had a seat at the table since its advent.

Less than fifty years after Justin had died, a new prolific writer was on the scene, and one that does not get as much credit as is due to him for the impact he has had on Christian thought, Tertullian. In his text *On the Resurrection and the Flesh*, Tertullian wrote,

> And so the flesh shall rise again, wholly in every man, in its own identity, in its absolute integrity. Wherever it may be, it is in safekeeping in God's presence, through that most faithful Mediator between God and man, (the man) Jesus Christ, who shall reconcile both God to man, and man to God; the spirit to the flesh, and the flesh to the spirit.[102]

What he is getting at is that mankind will be brought back in the flesh in a form of reconciliation of the flesh and the spirit, which also symbolizes the reconciliation of man to God. This is something that must be understood before moving on to the next topic. Mankind will live forever with God in new bodies, so long as they have made the one good choice, and that is the choice to follow Jesus Christ. The last answer that is given with regards to how this all comes together involves the fact that the Bible states that there will be eternal life.

The Life Everlasting

There certainly was a Jewish background to the ministry of Jesus, as He showed time and again the thought of eternal life with God as the main goal of those who would follow Him. Through looking at the Old Testament and comparing this with the New Testament texts, it is easily seen that was what the Messiah was to do. He was to usher in an eternal kingdom which would lead to everlasting life, and since it has been shown that this was clearly what Jesus thought that He was to accomplish in His life and ministry, it is not a far leap to garner the same understanding that Jesus had of the Old Testament and see how He was applying these verses within the context of His own ministry in the first century.

Old Testament

Job is possibly the first book of the Bible to have been composed, though scholars of the Old Testament are unsure. Nevertheless, Job provides an excellent picture of what hope in the redeemer should look like for those who believe that the Scriptures are giving the fullest picture of eternity. Job wrote,

> As for me, I know that my Redeemer lives, And at the last He will take His stand on the earth. Even after my skin is destroyed, Yet from my flesh I shall see God; Whom I myself shall behold, And whom my eyes will see and not another. My heart faints within me!
>
> Job 19:25–27

In saying all of this, the writer shows that there is life after death and that this time will be spent in the presence of the great Redeemer. Job talks about this happening in a future beyond what he could know by himself, as he states that his skin has been destroyed. This picture of eternity in the flesh shows a picture that is oft-repeated, even though this picture comes from as far back as any picture in the text of Scripture.

Daniel was apocalyptic in his writings, as God was giving him many visions of the time that was to come. Daniel recorded many future events, including the coming Messiah as well as the end of days prophecies. Referring back to Daniel 12:2, as covered previously, the eternal life that he spoke of was one in the flesh in the presence of God. He states that there will be those who will arise to eternal life with God and others that will arise to eternal judgment. The point of his writing is that whether in condemnation or in jubilation, those who are dead will rise again.

New Testament

As has already been noted, Jesus continued in the same vein as the prophets of old, showing that there was eternal life on the other side of the life that is being lived now. In one of the most famous discourses of the New Testament, Jesus is speaking to the Jewish teacher Nicodemus. Throughout this discourse, He is speaking of the eternal life that is to come. Jesus desired that Nicodemus would be able to understand how one came to have eternal life. He said,

> For God so loved the world, that He gave His only begotten Son, that whoever believes in Him shall not perish, but have eternal life. For God did not send the Son into the world to judge the world, but that the world might be saved through Him.
>
> John 3:16–17

First, Jesus says that the goal is to receive eternal life. Then Jesus follows that up by telling him the purpose of God sending the Son into the world. The key to this is understanding that the will of God is that none should perish. This is something that is carried over into the other books of the New Testament but is an inevitable conclusion for all of those who refuse to believe in what Jesus came to this earth to accomplish.

In much the same vein as that which was spoken by Jesus, Peter, in his second epistle, wrote, "The Lord is not slow about His promise, as some count slowness, but is patient toward you, not wishing for any to perish but for all to come to repentance" (2 Peter 3:9). This is to say that there is no reason to believe that the resurrection is not coming, just because it has not happened yet. There were those complaining in the middle of the first century, and every century since that, the Lord had not shown up yet, and this was a reason to leave the faith. Peter said that the Lord is not slow as some would count slowness, but that everything happens in due time. Another key point that he makes with regards to this is that there is an eternal life that awaits those who are in the faith. This is a key passage to showing that there is a need to continue in the faith until that day comes in which mankind will see the resurrection of the dead into eternal life. Peter would not be the last to espouse the belief in eternal life, as John covered this aspect in many places, passing this down to his own disciples, who would then continue this teaching down the chain of writers to the present day. The writers of the creed saw this as an essential teaching and one that must be held tightly to in order to be in the faith.

Church Fathers

Throughout the first several centuries of the church, there were many attempts at subverting the truth that was being preached by the true church. In the second century, there was a movement that had gained some attention throughout the Roman Empire called Gnosticism. Towards the middle of the second century, there were many heavyweight battles over whether the Christians were correct about the teachings of Jesus or if the Gnostics were the ones who were correct. One of the men who took up the torch for the battle was Irenaeus, a third-generation Christian (he was a disciple of Polycarp, who was a disciple of John). In his writings against the heresy of the Gnostics, one of the Scriptures he relied on heavily was 1 Corinthians 15:53–54, using this passage thirteen times in his rebuttal to their beliefs.

Irenaeus reminded those who read his text of the eternity that awaits those who have accepted what the text of the Bible says, saying, "that they who believe in Him shall be incorruptible and not subject to suffering, and shall receive the kingdom of heaven."[103] The Gnostics viewed the becoming of imperishable as being like light flowing from darkness, whereas Irenaeus sought a more literal interpretation of the text, saying that the body would actually be made imperishable in heaven. This exhibits that the orthodox belief in Scriptures that was handed down from the disciples to their own disciples was that of an actual everlasting life and not something which is symbolic as was used by the Gnostics. Again this shows that the creed holds to what was considered to be the orthodox belief that has been held throughout the entire life of the church, from the earliest believers through today.

Amen

This is what has been used to signify the end of a prayer, hymn, or creed throughout Judaism, Islam, and Christianity. Amen or אָמֵן (*āmēn*) means "so be it." This word has nothing to do with gender and should not be confused as such. It is a word that shows trust that God is who He said that He is. This is used as a confirmatory conclusion that shows the trust that one is to put in God. That is the heart of the Apostles' Creed, though. While there is a great deal of evidence that there is one God in Trinity and Trinity in unity, there is faith that one must have that God is exactly who He says He is.

About the Author

Matt Bertels is a twenty-three-year veteran of the United States Naval submarine service. He received his bachelor's degree in Theology and a master's of Ministry from Apostolic Faith Bible Institute, a master's in Religious Education, and a master's of Divinity from Liberty University. After taking a couple of years off from school, he finished his PhD through Trinity College of the Bible and Theological Seminary, writing his major writing project on the use of the writings of the church fathers in defending the faith today. He is married to Rachael. They have five children: Samuel, Roselyn, Israel, Augustine, and Raelyn.

Bibliography

Print Resources

-, "A common quotation from 'Augustine'?." Accessed October 3, 2021. https://faculty.georgetown.edu/jod/augustine/quote.

The Book of Thomas the Contender, The Gnostic Society Library, Accessed October 4, 2021, http://gnosis.org/naghamm/bookt.html.

-. *Martyrdom of Polycarp: Ante-Nicene Fathers Volume I.* Sunrise, FL: Eternal Sun Books, 2017.

-. *The Pastor of Hermas: Ante-Nicene Fathers Volume II.* Sunrise, FL: Eternal Sun Books, 2017.

Albert, David. "On the Origin of Everything." March 23, 2012. https://www.nytimes.com/2012/03/25/books/review/a-universe-from-nothing-by-lawrence-m-krauss.html.

Andrews, Travis M. "John 3:16, sports and Aaron Hernandez", New York Times, May 5, 2017. Accessed from www.washingtonpost.com/news/morning-mix/wp/2017/05/05/john-316-sports-and-aaron-hernandez/.

Anselm. *The Major Works.* Edited by Brian Davies and G R. Evans. Oxford World's Classics. Oxford: Oxford University Press, 2008.

Athenagoras. *Plea for Christians: Ante-Nicene Fathers Volume II.* Sunrise, FL: Eternal Sun Books, 2017.

Augustine. *Concerning the City of God Against the Pagans.* London: Penguin Books, 2003.

Augustine. "On the Catechizing of the Uninstructed." In *Doctrinal Treatises of st. Augustine.* Translated by Philip Schaff. London: Aeterna Press, 2014.

Augustine. *On Faith and the Creed.* Accessed September 30, 2021. https://www.newadvent.org/fathers/1304.htm.

Augustine, Edmund Hill, and John E Rotelle. 2002. *On Genesis: On Genesis: A Refutation of the Manichees, Unfinished Literal*

Commentary on Genesis, the Literal Meaning of Genesis. Hyde Park, N.Y.: New City Press.

Bruce, F. F. *Paul: Apostle of the Heart Set Free.* Grand Rapids, MI: Wm. B. Eerdman's Publishing Company, 1994.

Bruce, F. F. *The Book of the Acts (New International Commentary on the New Testament).* Grand Rapids, MI: Wm. B. Eerdman's Publishing Company, 1954.

Caesar Augustus. "The Achievements of the Deified Augustus." Last modified September 15, 2021. https://www.livius.org/sources/content/augustus-res-gestae/.

Chilton, Bruce, and Craig A. Evans, eds. *Studying the Historical Jesus: Evaluations of the State of Current Research.* Leiden: E.J. Brill, 1994.

Clement. *First Epistle of Clement to the Corinthians: Ante-Nicene Fathers Volume I.* Sunrise, FL: Eternal Sun Books, 2017.

Clement of Alexandria. *Exhortation to the Heathen: Ante-Nicene Fathers Volume II.* Sunrise, FL: Eternal Sun Books, 2017.

Craig, William Lane. *Reasonable Faith: Christian Truth and Apologetics.* 3rd ed. Wheaton, Ill.: Crossway Books, 2008.

Cyprian. Epistle LXXIII: *Ante-Nicene Fathers Volume V.* Sunrise, FL: Eternal Sun Books, 2017.

Cyril of Jerusalem. *Lectures Xviii.* Translated by Philip Schaff. Unknown: Library of Alexandria, 2003. Amazon Kindle.

Edwards et al., "Death of Christ." JAMA March 21, 1986—Vol 255, No. 11.

Ehrman, Bart D. *Did Jesus Exist? The Historical Argument for Jesus of Nazareth.* New York: HarperOne, 2012.

Ehrman, Bart. *Lost Scriptures: Books That Did Not Make It Into the New Testament.* Oxford: Oxford University Press, 2005.

Eusebius, and Paul L. Maier. Eusebius—*the Church History: A New Translation with Commentary.* Grand Rapids, MI: Kregel Publications, 1999.

González, Justo L. *The Story of Christianity*. 2nd ed. New York: HarperCollins, 2010.

Graham, Daniel W., "Heraclitus," The Stanford Encyclopedia of Philosophy (Fall 2019 Edition), Edward N. Zalta (ed.), https://plato.stanford.edu/archives/fall2019/entries/heraclitus.

Habermas, Gary R. *The Historical Jesus: Ancient Evidence for the Life of Christ*. Joplin, Mo.: College Press Pub. Co., 1996.

Hadid, Diaa. "Bethlehem Artefact Predates Jesus." Accessed October 2, 2021. https://www.independent.ie/world-news/middle-east/bethlehem-artefact-predates-jesus-26856829.html.

Henry, Matthew. *Matthew Henry's Commentary on the Whole Bible: Wherein Each Chapter Is Summed up in Its Contents, Each Paragraph Reduced to Its Proper Heads, the Sense given, and Largely Illustrated with Practical Remarks and Observations, Genesis to Revelation*. Peabody, MA: Hendrickson Publishers, 2002.

Huffman, Douglas S. "The Historical Jesus of Ancient Unbelief." *Journal of the Evangelical Theological Society* 40, no. 4 (December 1997): 551-64.

Ignatius. *The Epistle to the Magnesians: Ante-Nicene Fathers Volume I*. Sunrise, FL: Eternal Sun Books, 2017.

Ignatius. *The Epistle to the Philadelphians: Ante-Nicene Fathers Volume I*. Sunrise, FL: Eternal Sun Books, 2017.

Ignatius. *Epistle to the Trallians: Ante-Nicene Fathers Volume I*. Sunrise, FL: Eternal Sun Books, 2017.

Ignatius. *Epistle to the Smyrnaeans: Ante-Nicene Fathers Volume I*. Sunrise, FL: Eternal Sun Books, 2017.

Irenaeus. *Against Heresies: With the Fragments That Remain from His Other Works*. Translated by John Keble. London: Crossreach Publications, 2018.

Jarus, Owen. "Ancient Burial Ground with 100 Tombs Found Near Biblical Bethlehem." Accessed October 2, 2021. https://www.livescience.com/53939-ancient-burial-ground-found-near-bethlehem.html.

Josephus. *The Works of Flavius Josephus*. Translated by William Whiston. Seattle: Amazon, 2015. Kindle.

Justin Martyr. *Dialogue with Trypho, Ante-Nicene Fathers Volume I*, Sunrise, FL: Eternal Sun Books, 2017. 231.

Justin Martyr. *On the Resurrection: Ante-Nicene Fathers Volume I*. Sunrise, FL: Eternal Sun Books, 2017.

Kelly, J N D. *Early Christian Creeds*. 3rd ed. London: Continuum, 2006.

Licona, Mike. *The Resurrection of Jesus: A New Historiographical Approach*. Downers Grove, Ill.: IVP Academic, 2010.

Lucian of Samosata. *The Death of Peregrine*. Retrieved from sacred-texts.com. Accessed October 1, 2021. https://www.sacred-texts.com/cla/luc/wl4/wl420.htm.

Lüdemann, Gerd. *The Resurrection of Christ: A Historical Inquiry*. Amherst, NY: Prometheus Books, 2004. Amazon Kindle.

Lüdemann, Gerd, and Alf Özen. *What Really Happened to Jesus: A Historical Approach to the Resurrection*. American ed. Louisville, Ky.: Westminster John Knox Press, 1995.

Macrobius. *Saturnalia*. Translated by Robert Kaster. Boston: Harvard University Press, 2011.

Maier, Paul. "Josephus and Jesus." North American Mission Board. Accessed October 1, 2021. https://www.namb.net/apologetics/resource/josephus-and-jesus/.

Mara bar Serapion. "Did Jesus Exist? Mara bar Serapion and the Talmud." Christian Apologetics Alliance. April 12, 2016. http://christianapologeticsalliance.com/2016/04/12/did-jesus-exist-part-5-mara-bar-serapion-the-talmud/.

Meyer, Stephen C. "Not By Chance" Discovery Institute, accessed December 12, 2020. https://www.discovery.org/a/3059/.

Mitra, Debala, and G Bhattacharya. Sri Garib Dass Oriental Series. Vol. 83, *Studies in Art and Archaeology of Bihar and Bengal:*

Nalinikānta Śatavārṣikī, Dr. N.K. Bhattasali Centenary Volume, 1888–1988. Delhi, India: Sri Satguru Publications, 1989.

Nelte, Frank W. "The Differences between 'create' and 'make' in Genesis 1." Accessed September 30, 2021. https://www.franknelte. net/article.php?article_id=173.

Novatian. *A Treatise Concerning the Trinity: Ante-Nicene Fathers Volume* V. Sunrise, FL: Eternal Sun Books, 2017.

Origen, *Commentary on the Gospel of Matthew*, Book X, chapter 17, https://www.newadvent.org/fathers/101610.htm, accessed January 2, 2021.

Origen. *De Principiis: Ante-Nicene Fathers Volume IV*. Sunrise, FL: Eternal Sun Books, 2017.

Origen. *The Works of Origen*. Seattle: Amazon, 2011. Kindle.

Paley, William. *Natural Theology*. United States: Coachwhip Publications, 2005.

Pliny the Younger. "Letters of Pliny the Younger and the Emperor Trajan." PBS Frontline. Accessed October 1, 2021. https://www.pbs. org/wgbh/pages/frontline/shows/religion/maps/primary/pliny. html.

Roth, Gustav. Sata-Pitaka series. Indo-Asian Literatures. Vol. 624, Stupa: *Cult and Symbolism*. New Delhi: International Academy of Indian Culture and, 2009.

Rufinus, Tyrannius. *A Commentary on the Apostles' Creed*. Translated by Ernest F. Morrison. London: Metuen & Co. LTD., 1916.

Seneca, Dialogue "To Marcia on Consolation," in Moral Essays, 6.20.3, trans. John W. Basore, The Loeb Classical Library (Cambridge, Mass.: Harvard University Press, 1946) 2:69.

Tacitus, Cornelius. *The Annals of Imperial Rome*. Rev. ed. Translated by Michael Grant. Penguin Classics. Harmondsworth Eng.: Penguin Books, 1973.

Tertullian. *Latin Christianity: It's Founder Tertullian*. Translated by Philip Schaff. Sunshine, FL: Eternal Sun Books, 2017.

Thayer, Joseph. *Thayer's Greek-English Lexicon of the New Testament*. 10th ed. Peabody, MA: Hendrickson Publishers, 2012.

Wiener, Norbert. *Cybernetics: Or, Control and Communication in the Animal and the Machine*. [second ed. Cambridge, Massachusetts: The MIT Press, 2019.

Video Resources

"Is There Evidence of Something Beyond Nature?"
https://youtu.be/F6rd4HEdffw.
Tim Tebow Shares Incredible Story of John 3:16,
https://www.youtube.com/watch?v=7WVnAbdHZao, accessed February 1, 2021.

Endnotes

[1] Irenaeus, *Against Heresies: With the Fragments That Remain from His Other Works*, trans. John Keble (London: Crossreach Publications, 2018), 18.

[2] Justo L. González, *The Story of Christianity*, 2nd ed. (New York: HarperCollins, 2010), 74.

[3] Augustine, "On Faith and the Creed," accessed September 30, 2021, https://www.newadvent.org/fathers/1304.htm.

[4] J. N. D. Kelly, Early Christian Creeds, 3rd ed. (London: Continuum, 2006), 101.

[5] All Scripture cited is from the New American Standard Bible (Lockman Foundation) 1995 unless otherwise noted.

[6] William Paley, *Natural Theology* (United States: Coachwhip, 2005), 16.

[7] Irenaeus, *Against Heresies: With the Fragments That Remain from His Other Works*, 47.

[8] Anselm, *The Major Works*, ed. Brian Davies and G R. Evans, Oxford World's Classics (Oxford: Oxford University Press, 2008), 112.

[9] William Lane Craig, *Reasonable Faith: Christian Truth and Apologetics*, 3rd ed. (Wheaton, Ill.: Crossway Books, 2008), 172.

[10] Albert David, "On the Origin of Everything," March 23, 2012, https://www.nytimes.com/2012/03/25/books/review/a-universe-from-nothing-by-lawrence-m-krauss.html.

[11] Stephen C. Meyer, "Not By Chance" Discovery institute, https://www.discovery.org/a/3059/, accessed December 12, 2020.

[12] "Is There Evidence of Something Beyond Nature?" https://youtu.be/F6rd4HEdffw.

[13] Norbert Wiener, *Cybernetics: Or, Control and Communication in the Animal and the Machine*, [second ed. (Cambridge, Massachusetts: The MIT Press, 2019), 132.

[14] Frank W. Nelte, "The Differences between 'create' and 'make' in Genesis 1," accessed September 30, 2021, https://www.franknelte.net/article.php?article_id=173.

[15] Augustine, Edmund Hill, and John E. Rotelle, *On Genesis* (Hyde Park, NY: New City Press, 2002), 291.

[16] Debala Mitra and G Bhattacharya, Sri Garib Dass Oriental Series, vol. 83, Studies in Art and Archaeology of Bihar and Bengal: Nalinikānta Śatavārṣikī, Dr. N. K. Bhattasali Centenary Volume, 1888–1988 (Delhi, India: Sri Satguru Publications, 1989), 139.

[17] Gustav Roth, Sata-Pitaka series. Indo-Asian Literatures, vol. 624, *Stupa: Cult and Symbolism* (New Delhi: International Academy of Indian Culture and, 2009), 167.

[18] Origen, The Works of Origen (Seattle: Amazon, 2011), 17965, Kindle.

[19] Bart D. Ehrman, *Did Jesus Exist? The Historical Argument for Jesus of Nazareth* (New York: HarperOne, 2012), 177.

[20] Josephus, *The Works of Flavius Josephus*, trans. William Whiston (Seattle: Amazon, 2015), 2931, Kindle.

[21] Paul Maier, "Josephus and Jesus," North American Mission Board, accessed October 1, 2021, https://www.namb.net/apologetics/resource/josephus-and-jesus/.

[22] Origen, *Commentary on the Gospel of Matthew*, Book X, chapter 17, https://www.newadvent.org/fathers/101610.htm, accessed January 2, 2021.

[23] Douglas S. Huffman, "The Historical Jesus of Ancient Unbelief," *Journal of the Evangelical Theological Society* 40, no. 4 (December 1997): 551–64.

[24] Cornelius Tacitus, *The Annals of Imperial Rome*, rev. ed., trans. Michael Grant Penguin Classics (Harmondsworth Eng.: Penguin Books, 1973), 365.

[25] Pliny the Younger, "Letters of Pliny the Younger and the Emperor Trajan," PBS Frontline, accessed October 1, 2021, https://www.pbs.

org/wgbh/pages/frontline/shows/religion/maps/primary/pliny.html.

[26] Mara bar Serapion, "Did Jesus Exist? Mara bar Serapion and the Talmud," Christian Apologetics Alliance, April 12, 2016, http://christianapologeticsalliance.com/2016/04/12/did-jesus-exist-part-5-mara-bar-serapion-the-talmud/.

[27] Lucian of Samosota. *The Death of Peregrine*. Line 11-13. Retrieved from sacred-texts.com. Accessed October 1, 2021. https://www.sacred-texts.com/cla/luc/wl4/wl420.htm.

[28] Mike Licona, *The Resurrection of Jesus: A New Historiographical Approach* (Downers Grove, Ill.: IVP Academic, 2010), 245.

[29] Augustine, *Concerning the City of God Against the Pagans* (London: Penguin Books, 2003), 106.

[30] Jospeh Thayer, *Thayer's Greek-English Lexicon of the New Testament*, 10th ed. (Peabody, MA: Hendrickson Publishers, 2012), 672.

[31] This is seen through multiple sites regarding the learning of the Jewish faith. These sites all refer to the future coming of the Davidic king who will be sent to rule on this earth.

[32] Matthew presents many more proofs for the messianic prophecies than the other books of the New Testament as it appears to have been written as a polemic for the Jewish people to come to faith in the person of Jesus of Nazareth.

[33] Travis M. Andrews, "John 3:16, sports and Aaron Hernandez," New York Times, May 5, 2017. Accessed from www.washingtonpost.com/news/morning-mix/wp/2017/05/05/john-316-sports-and-aaron-hernandez/.

[34] Tim Tebow Shares Incredible Story of John 3:16, https://www.youtube.com/watch?v=7WVnAbdHZao, accessed February 1, 2021.

[35] Daniel W. Graham, "Heraclitus," The Stanford Encyclopedia of Philosophy (Fall 2019 Edition), Edward N. Zalta (ed.), https://

plato.stanford.edu/archives/fall2019/entries/heraclitus.

[36] Irenaeus, *Against Heresies: With the Fragments That Remain from His Other Works*, 123.

[37] Caesar Augustus, "The Achievements of the Deified Augustus," last modified September 15, 2021, https://www.livius.org/sources/content/augustus-res-gestae/.

[38] ibid.

[39] Origen, location 9144.

[40] Owen Jarus, "Ancient Burial Ground with 100 Tombs Found Near Biblical Bethlehem," accessed October 2, 2021, https://www.livescience.com/53939-ancient-burial-ground-found-near-bethlehem.html.

[41] Diaa Hadid, "Bethlehem Artefact Predates Jesus," accessed October 2, 2021, https://www.independent.ie/world-news/middle-east/bethlehem-artefact-predates-jesus-26856829.html.

[42] Justin Martyr, *Dialogue with Trypho, Ante-Nicene Fathers Volume I* (Sunrise, FL: Eternal Sun Books, 2017), 231.

[43] Ignatius, *Epistle to the Trallians: Ante-Nicene Fathers Volume I* (Sunrise, FL: Eternal Sun Books, 2017), 66.

[44] Macrobius, *Saturnalia*, trans. Robert Kaster (Boston: Harvard University Press, 2011), 349.

[45] Josephus, *Antiquities of the Jews*, 18.55-59.

[46] Ibid.

[47] Eusebius and Paul L. Maier, Eusebius—*the Church History: A New Translation with Commentary* (Grand Rapids, MI: Kregel Publications, 1999), 65.

[48] Bruce Chilton and Craig A. Evans, eds., *Studying the Historical Jesus: Evaluations of the State of Current Research* (Leiden: E.J. Brill, 1994), 465.

[49] Edwards et al, "Death of Christ." JAMA March 21, 1986—Vol 255, No. 11, p 1457.

[50] Seneca, Dialogue "To Marcia on Consolation," in Moral

Essays, 6.20.3, trans. John W. Basore, The Loeb Classical Library (Cambridge, Mass.: Harvard University Press, 1946) 2:69.

[51] David L. Balch and Carolyn Osiek, eds., *Early Christian Families in Context: An Interdisciplinary Dialogue* (Grand Rapids, Mich.: W.B. Eerdmans Pub. Co., 2003), 103.

[52] Ehrman, *Did Jesus Exist?*, 63.

[53] Tacitus, *Annals of Rome.*

[54] Mara bar Serapion.

[55] Edwards, et al., "On the Physical Death of Jesus Christ."

[56] This is noted by the case of Yohannan, the Jewish individual whose heel has the nail still in it, as it was found in 1968.

[57] This is taken from Qur'an, Surah 4, verses 157-158, which reads: "And [for] their saying, 'Indeed, we have killed the Messiah, Jesus, the son of Mary, the messenger of Allah.'" And they did not kill him, nor did they crucify him; but [another] was made to resemble him to them. And indeed, those who differ over it are in doubt about it. They have no knowledge of it except the following of assumption. And they did not kill him, for certain. Rather, Allah raised him to Himself. And ever is Allah Exalted in Might and Wise.

[58] Gerd Lüdemann, The Resurrection of Christ: A Historical Inquiry (Amherst, NY: Prometheus Books, 2004), 469, Amazon Kindle.

[59] Clement, *First Epistle of Clement to the Corinthians: Ante-Nicene Fathers Volume I* (Sunrise, FL: Eternal Sun Books, 2017), 10.

[60] Josephus, *Antiquities of the Jews*, 20.9.

[61] F. F. Bruce, *Paul: Apostle of the Heart Set Free* (Grand Rapids, MI: Wm. B. Eerdman's Publishing Company, 1994), 41.

[62] Clement, *First Epistle to the Corinthians*, 10.

[63] Gary R. Habermas, *The Historical Jesus: Ancient Evidence for the Life of Christ* (Joplin, Mo.: College Press Pub. Co., 1996), 157.

[64] Gerd Lüdemann and Alf Özen, *What Really Happened to Jesus: A Historical Approach to the Resurrection*, American ed. (Louisville,

Ky.: Westminster John Knox Press, 1995), 14-15.

[65] Justin Martyr, *Dialogue with Trypho*, 221.

[66] Qur'an 4:157-158, quran.com, accessed 8/13/21.

[67] *The Book of Thomas the Contender*, The Gnostic Society Library, Accessed October 4, 2021, http://gnosis.org/naghamm/bookt. html.

[68] Bart Ehrman, *Lost Scriptures: Books That Did Not Make It Into the New Testament* (Oxford: Oxford University Press, 2005), 122.

[69] Irenaeus, *Against Heresies: With the Fragments That Remain from His Other Works*, 79.

[70] Ibid., 199.

[71] Eusebius, *Church History*, 129.

[72] J. N. D. Kelly, in his *Commentary on the Pastoral Epistles*, stated that the execution of Paul cannot be dated before the persecution of Nero in 64/65 CE and, as such, puts Paul most likely in Rome up to this point. This provides the latest dating for Matthew at 65 CE, with Mark following shortly after their departure.

[73] Eusebius, *Church History*, 123.

[74] The Gallio inscription is a series of nine fragments from Emperor Claudius on the subject from a procounsul named Gallio who dismissed the charge brought by the Jews against Paul in Acts 18:12–17.

[75] Muratorian Fragment.

[76] Irenaeus, Against Heresies: *With the Fragments That Remain from His Other Works*, 89.

[77] Tertullian, *Latin Christianity: It's Founder Tertullian*, trans. Philip Schaff (Sunshine, FL: Eternal Sun Books, 2017), 280.

[78] F. F. Bruce, *The Book of the Acts (New International Commentary on the New Testament)*, (Eerdmans: Grand Rapids, MI, 2005), 166.

[79] Polycarp, *Epistle to the Ephesians: Ante-Nicene Fathers Volume I* (Sunrise, FL: Eternal Sun Books, 2017), 36.

[80] Matthew Henry, *Matthew Henry's Commentary on the Whole*

Bible: Wherein Each Chapter Is Summed up in Its Contents, Each Paragraph Reduced to Its Proper Heads, the Sense given, and Largely Illustrated with Practical Remarks and Observations, Genesis to Revelation (Peabody, MA: Hendrickson Publishers, 2002), 1771.

[81] Thayer, 105.

[82] Unknown, *The Pastor of Hermas: Ante-Nicene Fathers Volume II* (Sunrise, FL: Eternal Sun Books, 2017), 113

[83] Clement of Alexandria, *Exhortation to the Heathen: Ante-Nicene Fathers Volume II* (Sunrise, FL: Eternal Sun Books, 2017), 163.

[84] Origen, *De Principiis: Ante-Nicene Fathers Volume IV* (Sunrise, FL: Eternal Sun Books, 2017), 269.

[85] Athenagoras, *Plea for Christians: Ante-Nicene Fathers Volume II* (Sunrise, FL: Eternal Sun Books, 2017), 113.

[86] Novatian, *A Treatise Concerning the Trinity: Ante-Nicene Fathers Volume V* (Sunrise, FL: Eternal Sun Books, 2017), 554.

[87] Ignatius, *The Epistle to the Philadelphians: Ante-Nicene Fathers Volume I* (Sunrise, FL: Eternal Sun Books, 2017), 77.

[88] Origen, *De Principiis*, 241.

[89] Tertullian, *Against Praxeas: Latin Christianity: It's Founder Tertullian* (Sunrise, FL: Eternal Sun Books, 2017), 518.

[90] Cyprian, Epistle LXXIII: *Ante-Nicene Fathers Volume V* (Sunrise, FL: Eternal Sun Books, 2017) 340.

[91] Tyrannius Rufinus, A Commentary on the Apostles' Creed, trans. Ernest F. Morrison (London: Metuen & Co. LTD., 1916), 50.

[92] Ignatius, *The Epistle to the Smyrnaeans: Ante-Nicene Fathers Volume I* (Sunrise, FL: Eternal Sun Books, 2017), 83.

[93] -, *Martyrdom of Polycarp: Ante-Nicene Fathers Volume I* (Sunrise, FL: Eternal Sun Books, 2017), 39.

[94] Irenaeus, *Against Heresies*, 18.

[95] Cyril of Jerusalem, *Lectures Xviii*, trans. Philip Schaff (Unknown: Library of Alexandria, 2003), 1, Amazon Kindle.

[96] Ibid.

[97] Ignatius, *Letter to the Magnesians: Ante-Nicene Fathers Volume I* (Sunrise, FL: Eternal Sun Books, 2017), 59.

[98] "A common quotation from 'Augustine'?," accessed October 3, 2021, https://faculty.georgetown.edu/jod/augustine/quote.

[99] Augustine, "On the Catechizing of the Uninstructed," in *Doctrinal Treatises of st. Augustine*, trans. Philip Schaff (London: Aeterna Press, 2014), 494.

[100] Barnabas, *The Epistle of Barnabas: Ante-Nicene Fathers Volume I* (Sunrise, FL: Eternal Sun Books, 2017), 130.

[101] Justin Martyr, *On the Resurrection: Ante-Nicene Fathers Volume I* (Sunrise, FL: Eternal Sun Books, 2017), 266.

[102] Tertullian, *On the Resurrection of the Flesh: Latin Christianity: It's Founder Tertullian* (Sunrise, FL: Eternal Sun Books, 2017), 507.

[103] Irenaeus, Against Heresies, 145.

CPSIA information can be obtained
at www.ICGtesting.com
Printed in the USA
LVHW050335300122
709588LV00012B/459

9 781685 561178